OPPOSING
VIEWPOINTS®
SERIES

Stem Cells

Other Books of Related Interest:

Opposing Viewpoints Series
Biomedical Ethics
Medicine
Reproductive Technologies
Technology and Society

At Issue Series
Human Embryo Experimentation

"Congress shall make no law . . . abridging the freedom of speech, or of the press."

First Amendment to the U.S. Constitution

The basic foundation of our democracy is the First Amendment guarantee of freedom of expression. The Opposing Viewpoints Series is dedicated to the concept of this basic freedom and the idea that it is more important to practice it than to enshrine it.

OPPOSING
VIEWPOINTS®
SERIES

Stem Cells

Jacqueline Langwith, Book Editor

GREENHAVEN PRESS

An imprint of Thomson Gale, a part of The Thomson Corporation

THOMSON
™
GALE

Detroit • New York • San Francisco • New Haven, Conn. • Waterville, Maine • London

Christine Nasso, *Publisher*
Elizabeth Des Chenes, *Managing Editor*

© 2007 Thomson Gale, a part of The Thomson Corporation.

Thomson and Star logo are trademarks and Gale and Greenhaven Press are registered trademarks used herein under license.

For more information, contact:
Greenhaven Press
27500 Drake Rd.
Farmington Hills, MI 48331-3535
Or you can visit our Internet site at http://www.gale.com

LIBRARY OF CONGRESS CATALOGING-IN-PUBLICATION DATA

Stem cells / Jacqueline Langwith, book editor.
        p. cm. -- (Opposing viewpoints)
    Includes bibliographical references and index.
    ISBN-13: 978-0-7377-3648-9 (hardcover) -- ISBN-13: 978-0-7377-3649-6 (pbk.)
    1. Stem cells--Research--Moral and ethical aspects. 2. Embryonic stem cells--Research--Moral and ethical aspects. I. Langwith, Jacqueline.
    QH588.S83S7448 2007
    174.2'8--dc22
                                                                        2007002991

ISBN-10: 0-7377-3648-8 (hardcover)
ISBN-10: 0-7377-3649-6 (pbk.)

Printed in the United States of America
10 9 8 7 6 5 4 3 2 1

Contents

Chapter 3: What Role Should the Government Play in Stem Cell Research?

Chapter 4: Are There Alternatives to Embryonic Stem Cells?

Why Consider Opposing Viewpoints?

> "The only way in which a human being can make some approach to knowing the whole of a subject is by hearing what can be said about it by persons of every variety of opinion and studying all modes in which it can be looked at by every character of mind. No wise man ever acquired his wisdom in any mode but this."
>
> *John Stuart Mill*

In our media-intensive culture it is not difficult to find differing opinions. Thousands of newspapers and magazines and dozens of radio and television talk shows resound with differing points of view. The difficulty lies in deciding which opinion to agree with and which "experts" seem the most credible. The more inundated we become with differing opinions and claims, the more essential it is to hone critical reading and thinking skills to evaluate these ideas. Opposing Viewpoints books address this problem directly by presenting stimulating debates that can be used to enhance and teach these skills. The varied opinions contained in each book examine many different aspects of a single issue. While examining these conveniently edited opposing views, readers can develop critical thinking skills such as the ability to compare and contrast authors' credibility, facts, argumentation styles, use of persuasive techniques, and other stylistic tools. In short, the Opposing Viewpoints series is an ideal way to attain the higher-level thinking and reading skills so essential in a culture of diverse and contradictory opinions.

In addition to providing a tool for critical thinking, Opposing Viewpoints books challenge readers to question their own strongly held opinions and assumptions. Most people form their opinions on the basis of upbringing, peer pressure, and personal, cultural, or professional bias. By reading carefully balanced opposing views, readers must directly confront new ideas as well as the opinions of those with whom they disagree. This is not to simplistically argue that everyone who reads opposing views will—or should—change his or her opinion. Instead, the series enhances readers' understanding of their own views by encouraging confrontation with opposing ideas. Careful examination of others' views can lead to the readers' understanding of the logical inconsistencies in their own opinions, perspective on why they hold an opinion, and the consideration of the possibility that their opinion requires further evaluation.

Evaluating Other Opinions

To ensure that this type of examination occurs, Opposing Viewpoints books present all types of opinions. Prominent spokespeople on different sides of each issue as well as well-known professionals from many disciplines challenge the reader. An additional goal of the series is to provide a forum for other, less known, or even unpopular viewpoints. The opinion of an ordinary person who has had to make the decision to cut off life support from a terminally ill relative, for example, may be just as valuable and provide just as much insight as a medical ethicist's professional opinion. The editors have two additional purposes in including these less known views. One, the editors encourage readers to respect others' opinions—even when not enhanced by professional credibility. It is only by reading or listening to and objectively evaluating others' ideas that one can determine whether they are worthy of consideration. Two, the inclusion of such viewpoints encourages the important critical thinking skill of objectively evaluating an author's credentials and bias. This evaluation will illuminate an author's reasons for taking a particular stance on an issue and will aid in readers' evaluation of the author's ideas.

It is our hope that these books will give readers a deeper understanding of the issues debated and an appreciation of the complexity of even seemingly simple issues when good and honest people disagree. This awareness is particularly important in a democratic society such as ours in which people enter into public debate to determine the common good. Those with whom one disagrees should not be regarded as enemies but rather as people whose views deserve careful examination and may shed light on one's own.

Thomas Jefferson once said that "difference of opinion leads to inquiry, and inquiry to truth." Jefferson, a broadly educated man, argued that "if a nation expects to be ignorant and free . . . it expects what never was and never will be." As individuals and as a nation, it is imperative that we consider the opinions of others and examine them with skill and discernment. The Opposing Viewpoints series is intended to help readers achieve this goal.

David L. Bender and Bruno Leone,
Founders

Introduction

"When Dolly was born, even I got caught up in the hype. During the initial brouhaha, I found myself telling one reporter that Dolly "might reasonably claim to be the most extraordinary creature ever born."

Ian Wilmut,
English embryologist with leading
role in the first successful cloning
of a mammal

"We derived a few cell lines, and that's kind of neat, but what I anticipated is that there would be this media storm that would last, I don't know, three to six months. And then people would just get on with their lives and do something else, because they have short attention spans. But it's seven years in now, and it's still this lively topic of discussion."

James Thomson,
cell biologist and pioneer in the
field of stem cell research

Current debates about stem cells can be traced back to two scientific discoveries made in the late 1990s. First, on July 5, 1996, researchers in Scotland witnessed the birth of a very special lamb named Dolly. Months earlier they had painstakingly created her from an udder cell of an adult sheep. Dolly was the first mammal cloned from an adult cell, and her arrival caused a sensation the world over. The second discovery came two years later and across the Atlantic Ocean. In the fall of 1998, a team of researchers at the University of Wisconsin announced that they had extracted stem cells from a human embryo and had been able to keep the cells alive and growing in a petri dish. Examining the historical significance of these two scientific discoveries is important to understanding the stem cell debate.

In 1996, Ian Wilmut, considered the father of Dolly, turned scientific dogma on its head. Before Dolly was born most scientists thought that mammals could never be cloned because the adult cells of species that undergo sexual reproduction lack a characteristic called totipotency, which allows the regeneration of an entire organism from a single cell. Taking a cutting of an ivy plant, for instance, placing it in a jar of water, and eventually growing an entire plant is dependent on totipotency. Adult animal cells do not normally possess totipotency, mostly because animal cells differentiate into hundreds of specialized cell types, such as brain cells, heart cells, and muscle cells. Scientists thought it impossible to regenerate an entire animal from a single cell. Ian Wilmut and a team of scientists at the Roslin Institute near Edinburgh, Scotland, however, discovered a way to do just that. Using a single cell from the udder of an adult Finn Dorset sheep and an egg cell from another sheep, and using a procedure called "somatic cell nuclear transfer" (SCNT), they were able to create a clone of the Finn Dorset sheep, which they named Dolly. In 2006, Wilmut noted, "While we now take for granted that it is possible to clone adult animals, the birth of Dolly shocked those in the general public who dwelled on the implications of reproduction without the act of sex. The feat shocked many in the research community, too. Scientists were apt to declare that this or that procedure would be 'biologically impossible,' but with Dolly that expression lost all meaning." Dolly was photographed, written about, and filmed by reporters and photographers from all over the world. According to Wilmut, Dolly seemed to know she was a celebrity—sometimes acting like a woolly prima donna. Since 1996, many other animals have been cloned via the SCNT procedure, including cattle, goats, pigs, dogs, cats, and mice; however, no one has so far reported the successful cloning of a human embryo.

A human embryo, whether it comes into existence via cloning or via the union of sperm and egg, begins the process of development as a single cell. Immediately, the single cell begins dividing and replicating. At five days old a human embryo, at this stage called a blastocyst, is about the size of the period at the end of this sentence. It is made up of about two hundred cells, some of which are pluripotent stem cells, meaning, the cells can specialize and change into one of more than two hundred different types of cells found in the human body. Extracting and culturing stem cells from human embryos was a coveted goal of scientists for many years prior to 1998. They were inspired and excited by the capability of embryonic stem cells to become any type of cell in the human body and wanted to study them and possibly use them to replace injured or diseased cells in humans. But in order to use and study the cells, scientists needed to find a way to nurture them and keep them alive once they were removed from the embyro.

Growing cells in artificial media is a challenging process. Cells can be fickle, and scientists needed to find just the right nutrient broth to grow them in. A skosh more phosphorous or a smidge more glucose meant the difference between success and failure. In 1998, James Thomson and a group of researchers found just the right mixture and just the right technique to extract stem cells from a human embryo and to grow the cells and keep them alive. Their results were published in the scientific journal *Science* in November of that year. Another group, led by John Gearhart at the Johns Hopkins School of Medicine in Baltimore also extracted and cultured embryonic stem cells, but using a different technique.

Immediately, the exciting medical and research potential as well as the ethical implications of their accomplishment were recognized by scientists and nonscientists alike. But the vast potential of human embryonic stem cells does not come without a cost: a human embryo. Thomson used an embryo that had been created via in vitro fertilization (IVF) at a fertility clinic. The parents of the embryo had already achieved a successful pregnancy and chose to donate unneeded embryos for research instead of discarding them. In interviews in 2004 and 2005, James Thomson commented on the morality of using the embryos and on the therapeutic potential of embryonic stem cells. "Regardless of what you think the moral status of those embryos is, it makes sense to me that it's a better moral decision to use them to help people than just to throw them out. I think human embryonic stem cells have this tremendous potential; the specifics of that potential are difficult to predict, but scientists are very rarely wrong when they think something is important."

Ian Wilmut and James Thomson's discoveries hinted at a brave new world of medical possibilities. By using the SCNT procedure to produce human embryos genetically matched to patients and using the techniques developed by Thomson to grow human embryonic stem cells, scientists hope one day to be able to replace or regenerate failing human cells and tissues without the complication of tissue rejection. They also hope to be able to study the mechanisms underlying human development and virtually every genetic disease that affects humans. In *Opposing Viewpoints: Stem Cells*, the contributors explore the stem cell issue in the following chapters: Will Stem Cells Cure Disease?, What Ethical and Moral Questions Surround Stem Cell Research?, What Role Should the Government Play in Stem Cell Research?, and Are There Alternatives to Embryonic Stem Cells? The discussions and debates about stem cell research began the moment Dolly was born and the moment Thomson grew those first embryonic stem cells. The viewpoints presented in this book are all connected in one way or another to these two discoveries.

CHAPTER 1

Will Stem Cells Cure Disease?

Chapter Preface

Fifteen years before stem cell research came into the spotlight, there was another medical technology that inspired hope for miraculous cures and stirred emotional ethical debates—gene therapy. But gene therapy has never realized its potential. It suffered a serious blow when a young patient named Jesse Gelsinger volunteered to participate in clinical trails and died as a result of the experimental treatment. As Sheryl Stolberg, a *New York Times* reporter who investigated and wrote about Jesse's death, wrote, "Every realm of medicine has its defining moment, often with a human face attached. Polio had Jonas Salk. In vitro fertilization had Louise Brown, the world's first test-tube baby. Transplant surgery had Barney Clark, the Seattle dentist with the artificial heart. AIDS had Magic Johnson. Now gene therapy has Jesse Gelsinger." Some people are pointing to the death of Jesse Gelsinger as a reason to move cautiously in stem cell research. Jesse Gelsinger's death highlights what can happen when researchers become obsessed with research success, especially when the research has such promise, at the expense of the very people they are hoping to help.

Jesse Gelsinger was an eighteen-year-old Arizona teenager with a rare metabolic disorder called ornithine transcarbamylase (OTC) deficiency. Jesse controlled his disease by eating a low-protein diet and taking over thirty pills every day. He signed up for experimental treatment at the University of Pennsylvania to test the efficacy of using gene therapy to treat infants with a fatal form of OTC. The results of the experiment were unlikely to help him. He knew this but wanted to proceed anyway. He told a friend, "What's the worst that can happen to me? I die, and it's for the babies."

Tragically, the worst did happen to Jesse. His doctors used a genetically altered adenovirus, which is the virus that causes the common cold, to deliver a healthy version of OTC to Jesse's liver. In gene therapy patients are given a healthy replacement of a defective or missing gene using a vector (something that can get inside the patient's genome) as a delivery vehicle to get the healthy gene to where it is needed in the patient's body. Because of their simple genetic makeup, viruses are the most commonly used vectors. Patients are infected with a virus that has had its pathogenic genes cut out and replaced with the gene the patient needs. Instead of causing a viral sickness the virus delivers a healthy copy of the needed gene. Jesse's doctors were hoping the healthy OTC gene would get incorporated into Jesse's genome and maybe he could discard some of his thirty or so pills; however, Jesse died four days later. The official cause of death was listed as respiratory distress syndrome. His doctors expected that Jesse would get a mild case of the common cold. Instead, he suffered a severe immune response and multiple organ failure. His liver shut down, then his kidneys, his lungs, and finally his brain. No one knows exactly why, but Jesse's immune system went haywire in response to the adenovirus. The federal government quickly reacted to Jesse's death and immediately halted all gene therapy trials until the reasons for Jesse's death could be revealed.

After a thorough investigation, the federal government charged the lead researchers in Jesse's therapy with disobeying several government regulations. It seems they were so confident of success and so obsessed with getting results that they had failed to inform the federal government of previous incidents where the adenovirus caused serious side effects and death. They neglected to mention this to Jesse, too. The government concluded that they had failed to tell the young man about all the risks involved in the experimental treatment. Additionally, it was found that based on pretrial liver screening, Jesse probably should have been excluded from the study in the first place.

Jesse Gelsinger's death was felt deeply by everyone in the gene therapy research community, and the impact of his death on medical research continues to this day. The U.S. National Institutes of Health and the Food and Drug Administration toughened the rules about the way patients are recruited into medical trials. As a result of Jesse's death there are greater protections for people participating in clinical research trials today.

As stem cell research progresses toward clinical trials—with the precautions taken in response to Jesse Gelsinger's death making it safer for people to participate—many people, including the contributors in the following chapter, are discussing whether stem cell research will ever achieve its promise to cure disease.

> *"Most scientists find stem cell therapy so promising that they believe it is only a matter of time before its use becomes routine."*

Stem Cells Will Soon Provide Cures for Many Diseases

Stem Cell Research Foundation

In the following viewpoint, the Stem Cell Research Foundation presents an optimistic outlook toward stem cell therapy that suggests that in the very near future such research will be used to provide dramatic cures for devastating illnesses. The foundation describes how embryonic stem cells cultured in the lab can be transplanted into people in a process similar to organ transplantation. The transplanted stem cells can replace damaged cells in diabetics, people with spinal cord injuries, and people who suffer from many other diseases. Despite challenges, the group asserts that stem cell therapy will soon become commonplace. The Stem Cell Research Foundation is a nonprofit organization that supports and promotes stem cell therapy research.

As you read, consider the following questions:

1. What is the definition of "stem cell therapy," according to the author?

Stem Cell Research Foundation, "Stem Cell Research: A Revolution in Medicine." www.stemcellresearchfoundation.org. Reproduced by permission.

2. What are "terminally differentiated cells?"

3. Name two challenges that must be overcome before stem cell therapy becomes commonplace.

Medicine today is moving rapidly toward the development of more effective cures for a host of diseases. In the past, doctors could usually only treat the symptoms of illness—treatments rarely addressed the causes. Today, many of the cures being developed by scientists are based on advanced techniques that target the root cause of disease rather than simply treating the symptoms. One of those techniques is called stem cell therapy.

What Is Stem Cell Therapy?

Stem cell therapy can be defined as a group of new techniques, or technologies, that rely on replacing diseased or dysfunctional cells with healthy, functioning ones. These new techniques are being applied experimentally to a wide range of human disorders, including many types of cancer, neurological diseases such as Parkinson's disease and ALS (Lou Gehrig's Disease), spinal cord injuries, heart disease and diabetes. Even blinding diseases of the retina may someday be cured by replacing dead retinal cells with new ones. To understand how stem cell therapy works, it helps to understand the role of cells in the body.

The Function of Cells

Cells are the basic building blocks of the human body. These tiny structures compose the skin, muscles, bones and all of the internal organs. They also hold many of the keys to how our bodies function. Cells serve both a structural and a functional role, performing an almost endless variety of actions to sustain the body's tissues and organs. The healthy functioning of all our cells is crucial to the maintenance of health. There are hundreds of different specialized cell types in the adult body. All of these cells perform very specific functions for the tissue or organ they compose. For example, specialized cells in the heart muscle "beat" rhythmically through the conduction of electrical and chemical signals, while the cells of the pancreas produce insulin to help the body convert food to energy. These mature cells have been differentiated, or dedicated, to performing their special tasks. Conventional wisdom has long maintained that under normal conditions, once a cell has become specialized, it cannot be changed into a different type of cell.

Like the body itself, cells have a finite life span; they eventually die. Most of the body's cells divide and duplicate throughout life, but some cells either don't replenish themselves or do so in such small numbers that they cannot replace themselves fast enough to combat disease. This is true for the cells of the brain and the heart, for example. In diseases like heart disease and Parkinson's, the death of cells overtakes the body's ability to replace them, and this eventually results in the failure of the organ.

How Does Stem Cell Therapy Work?

While cells are indispensable in performing vital functions for the body, they can also exist outside the body. They can live and divide in "cultures," or special solutions in test tubes or petri dishes. This ability of certain cell types to live isolated from other cells under controlled conditions has allowed scientists to study them independently of the organ or system they are normally a part of. Through the isolation and manipulation of cells, scientists are finding ways to identify young, regenerating ones that can be used to replace damaged or dead cells in diseased organs. This therapy is similar to the process of organ transplant, only the treatment consists of the transplantation of cells rather than organs. The cells that have shown by far the most promise of supplying diseased organs with healthy new cells are called stem cells.

Stem Cells Are Highly Versatile Cells

Simply put, stem cells are "primitive" cells, made early in an organism's development, that give rise to other types of cells. Also called progenitor cells, there are several kinds of stem cells. Totipotent cells are considered the "master" cells of the body because they contain all the genetic information needed to create all the cells of the body plus the placenta, which sustains the human embryo. Human cells have this capacity only during the first few divisions of a fertilized egg. After 3-4 divisions of totipotent cells, there follows a series of stages in which the cells become increasingly specialized.

The next stage of development produces pluripotent cells, which are highly versatile and can give rise to any cell type except the cells of the placenta. At the next stage, cells become multipotent, meaning they can give rise to several other cell types, but those types are limited in number. An example of multipotent cells is hematopoietic cells—blood stem cells that can develop into several types of blood cells, but cannot develop into brain cells. At the end of the long chain of cell divisions that make up the embryo are "terminally differentiated" cells—cells that are considered to be permanently committed to a specific function.

Scientists have long held the opinion that differentiated cells cannot be altered or caused to behave in any way other than the way in which they have been naturally committed. New research, however, has called that assumption into question. In recent experiments, scientists have been able to persuade blood stem cells to behave like neurons, or brain cells. Scientists now believe that stem cell research could reveal far more vital information about our bodies than was previously known.

In addition, it was recently discovered that some stem cells also occur in the bodies of adults, rather than exclusively in embryos. Many kinds of multipotent stem cells have been discovered in adults, and scientists believe that many more will be discovered. Research is now being conducted on both adult and embryonic stem cells to determine the characteristics and potential of both to cure disease. . . .

Stem Cell Therapy Is Building Toward Its Potential

Even though most of the work done in this field has been experimental, most scientists find stem cell therapy so promising that they believe it is only a matter of time before its use becomes routine. And while many of the hoped-for uses of cell therapy sound futuristic, there are a few forms of this technique that have already been in use for years. Bone marrow transplants are an example of cell therapy in which the stem cells in a donor's marrow are used to replace the blood cells of the victims of leukemia and other cancers. Cell therapy is also being used in experiments to graft new skin cells to treat serious burn victims, and to grow new corneas for the sight-impaired. In all of these uses, the goal is for the healthy cells to become integrated into the body and begin to function like the patient's own cells.

So far, the results of such experiments have exceeded expectations. In a recent advance, pancreatic cells were implanted into the body of a diabetic and began to produce insulin. Even though cell therapy is a new science, early results like these have caused great optimism in the scientific community. However, there are several scientific challenges that must be overcome before we can truly harness the power of stem cells.

What Are Some of the Challenges?

One of the first challenges that must be overcome for stem cell therapies to become more commonplace is the difficulty of identifying stem cells in tissue cultures, which contain numerous types of cells. While scientists are discovering new cell types almost every day, they estimate that there could literally be hundreds of human cell types. The process of identifying any desired type of stem cell will involve painstaking research. Second, once stem cells are identified and isolated, the right biochemical solution must be developed to cause these progenitor cells to differentiate into the desired cell types. This too will require a great deal of experimentation.

Assuming that the above obstacles have been overcome, new issues arise when the cells are implanted into a person. The cells must be integrated into the patient's own tissues and organs and "learn" to function in concert with the body's natural cells. Cardiac cells that beat in a cell culture, for example, may not beat in rhythm with a patient's own heart cells. And neurons injected into a damaged brain must become "wired into" the brain's intricate network of cells and their connections in order to function properly.

Yet another challenge is the phenomenon of tissue rejection. Just as in organ transplants, the body's immune cells will recognize transplanted cells as "foreign," setting off an immune reaction that could cause the transplant to fail and possibly endanger the patient. Cell recipients would have to take drugs to suppress their immune systems, which in itself could be dangerous.

Yet another concern is the possible risk of cancer. Cancer results when cells lose their internal "brakes" and keep dividing when further proliferation is no longer desirable. Researchers must find a delicate balance between fostering the growth of new cells to replenish damaged tissues and making sure that cells don't overgrow and become cancerous. However, most scientists believe that, with the appropriate research, these obstacles can be overcome and the power of stem cells can be harnessed.

Stem Cells Have the Potential to Revolutionize Medicine

Despite the many challenges before us, many scientists believe that stem cell therapy will revolutionize medicine. With the use of stem cell therapies, we may soon have dramatic cures for cancer, heart failure, Parkinson's disease, muscular dystrophy, diabetes, kidney disease, multiple sclerosis and a host of other diseases. Stem cell therapies have also shown great promise in helping to repair catastrophic spinal injuries, helping victims of paralysis regain movement, and repairing severe brain injury following a stroke. It is even possible that the human life span could be greatly extended due to the replenishment of tissues in aging organs. We may even have the ability one day to grow out our own organs for transplantation from our own stem cells, eliminating the danger of rejection. While we will undoubtedly encounter the limits of cell therapy one day, there is every reason to hope that this revolutionary new approach will result in radically improved ways to treat disease.

"*Stem cell science is no stranger to claims that don't stack up, results that can't be replicated and doctors willing to rush into the clinic.*"

The Promise of Stem Cells Is Exaggerated

Peter Aldhous

In the following viewpoint, Peter Aldhous presents evidence to show that the promise of stem cell research is nowhere near reality. Scientists' claims of cures and advances using both embryonic and adult stem cells are more hype than fact, he contends, and are merely a result of the media frenzy and political interest in the research. Aldhous argues that stem cell research science is fraught with unmet promises, claims that cannot be proven, and truth stretched thin. Peter Aldhous, bureau chief of New Scientist, *an international science and technology news weekly, writes extensively about stem cell research and other biomedical topics.*

As you read, consider the following questions:

1. When did reports first start appearing that adult stem cells could turn into all kinds of tissue, according to Aldhous?

Peter Aldhous, "Miracle Postponed: In the Light of the Korean Scandal, Many Big Claims about Stem Cells Are Looking Decidedly Doubtful," *New Scientist*, vol. 189, March. 11, 2006, pp. 38–41. Copyright © 2006 Reed Elsevier Business Publishing, Ltd. Reproduced by permission.

2. What happened to Jesse Gelsinger, as reported by the author?

3. According to Aldhous, why must embryonic stem cells be turned into a specific cell before they are transplanted into people?

Ayeoni Kim believed. He had been paralysed at just 8 years old when he was hit by a car on his way home from school. So when South Korea's science superstar, Woo Suk Hwang, asked if his team could take skin cells from Kim and use them to obtain stem cells that might one day provide a cure, Kim and his family were delighted. When Hwang visited him in hospital in April 2003, the boy, then 9, asked him if he would walk again. "I promise," Hwang replied.

Rash Promises

That promise became immortalised in a Korean postage stamp showing a man rising from his wheelchair. But it was always highly questionable. Even if Hwang had managed to derive cloned embryonic stem cells (ESCs) from the skin cells of Kim and 10 others—as he claimed in May 2005—he would still have been a long way from mending Kim's spinal cord. Cloning merely provides ESCs that will not be rejected by a patient's immune system. Whether cells derived from them could ever fix a spinal injury, especially an old one like Kim's, is far from clear.

Not only was Hwang's promise rash, we know now that he did not even clear the first hurdle when it came to fulfilling it. The evidence of cloned ESCs was fabricated, and his scientific papers have been retracted. This was fraud piled on hype. Yet Kim's family still cling to hope. "We told him, yes, one day you will walk again," Kim's father told the *Los Angeles Times* in January [2006]. "But you might have to wait a little longer."

Stem Cell Field Fraught with Difficulties

Stem cell biologists have been quick to dismiss Hwang as an aberration. They stress that their field has immense medical promise, which is true. But how close is that promise to being realised? Looked at in the grim light of the Hwang affair, an uncomfortable truth becomes apparent: stem cell science is no stranger to claims that don't stack up, results that can't be replicated and doctors willing to rush into the clinic.

"It is common knowledge that the bar for publication in this field often has appeared remarkably low," wrote David Shaywitz, an endocrinologist at the Harvard Stem Cell Institute, in an article in the *Washington Post* in January. "The result of this frenzy has been an entire body of literature that is viewed with extreme skepticism."

Many leading stem cell scientists agree with Shaywitz's damning assessment. "Things are not reproduced. You really wonder what's going on," says Gordon Keller of the Mount Sinai School of Medicine in New York City, president of the International Society for Stem Cell Research.

Despite the Hwang scandal, most stem cell scientists believe outright fraud is not a major issue. Some argue that teething problems are common in any new area of science, particularly if researchers let their enthusiasm get the better of them. Part of the problem may be that interpreting the results of stem cell experiments requires mastery of a variety of complex techniques, so researchers occasionally convince themselves they are seeing things that aren't really there. "What you're looking at is a hot field that attracts people who are not trained to jump in," says Irving Weissman, a veteran stem cell biologist at Stanford University in California.

Political Hyperbole and Media Hype

The unprecedented political and media spotlight on stem cell research has also contributed. As self-styled "pro-life" groups have lobbied against work on human ESCs, which are usually derived by destroying embryos just a few days old, scientists have been forced to champion this research or risk losing the right to carry it out. Meanwhile, hints that the "adult" stem cells found in many of our tissues might be more versatile than was thought have been seized upon by opponents of research on ESCs. This feverish debate has seen those on both sides make statements that they have later come to regret.

Adult Stem Cell Claims

The upshot is that scientists, politicians and activists of various persuasions have been making a great deal of some very shaky findings. Take some of the claims about the "plasticity" of adult stem cells. Unlike ESCs, which can develop into any of the body's tissues, adult stem cells were traditionally thought to replenish only one type of tissue. In the late 1990s, however, reports started appearing claiming that some adult stem cells could turn into all kinds of tissues. If true, there might be no need for ESCs.

Yet many of these findings, including some published in the most prominent scientific journals, have proved extremely difficult to repeat. And if other groups do not get the same results despite many attempts, something is clearly wrong.

Unreproducible Results

In a 1999 paper in *Science*, for example, researchers led by Angelo Vescovi, now at the San Raffaele Hospital in Milan, Italy, described how they irradiated mice to kill their bone marrow, which contains the stem cells that replenish blood cells.

They then injected the mice with neural stem cells taken from the brains of other mice. These neural stem cells apparently replaced the bone marrow stem cells that had been destroyed by the radiation, giving rise to a variety of blood cell types.

Other researchers have failed to replicate the experiment. According to Weissman, the results were always perplexing.

Fabricated Research

South Korean researcher Hwang Woo-suk resigned from his university on Friday [Dec. 23, 2005,] after the school said he fabricated stem-cell research that had raised hopes of new cures for hard-to-treat diseases.

A university panel, releasing initial findings of a probe, accused Hwang of damaging the scientific community with his deception, while South Korea's government rued the scandal surrounding the country's star scientist and said it may pull its funding for his research.

"I sincerely apologize to the people for creating a shock and disappointment," Hwang told reporters as he was leaving his office at Seoul National University, considered the country's top institution of higher learning.

"With an apologetic heart . . . I step down as professor," he said.

Associated Press, December 23, 2005. www.msnbc.com.

The blood cells apparently derived from the neural stem cells did not turn up in the animals' circulation for over 20 weeks. "Then suddenly, the whole system came from nowhere," says Weissman.

A 2002 paper in *Nature*, from Catherine Verfaillie's team at the University of Minnesota in Minneapolis, also attracted much attention. As reported a few months earlier by *New Scientist*, Verfaillie claimed a rare type of bone marrow stem cell could differentiate into almost any kind of tissue. Unsurprisingly, campaigners against embryo research championed the cells as a morally acceptable alternative to ESCs.

Since then, a company called Athersys in Cleveland, Ohio, has refined methods for extracting similar cells and hopes to begin trials to treat patients with heart disease in 2007. Academic groups, however, have had mixed success in trying to repeat Verfaillie's results. Even her own team was unable to isolate new cultures of the cells over a period of more than six months in late 2003 and early 2004.

Perhaps the biggest controversy surrounds a 2001 paper in *Nature*. Piero Anversa's team at New York Medical College in Valhalla described experiments in mice in which bone marrow cells repaired the damage caused by a heart attack by forming new heart muscle. Two teams, one led by Weissman, the other by Chuck Murry of the University of Washington in Seattle, have since tried without success to replicate the findings. "We failed miserably," says Murry.

Clinical Trials: Mixed Results amid Concerns

That has not deterred doctors from trying the therapy in people. Several clinical trials are under way on both sides of the Atlantic. So far, the results have been mixed. While heart function has improved in some patients, there is no firm evidence that this is due to transplanted cells forming new muscle tissue. Instead, the bone marrow cells might have temporarily boosted the natural healing process by releasing chemical signals, or by causing local inflammation. "Perhaps we don't need cells at all," says Murry.

Given that nobody really knows what is going on, Murry is not alone in thinking that it was unwise to start clinical trials so soon. No serious safety problems have so far arisen in the cardiac trials, but stem cell biologists worry that rushing into the clinic on the basis of unreplicated findings could end in disaster. Their nightmare scenario is a repeat of the 1999 Jesse Gelsinger tragedy, in which an 18-year-old volunteer with a liver disease died from an inflammatory reaction to the virus used to deliver genes. The case cast a pall over the field of gene therapy that remains to this day.

Stemness Is Elusive

So why have some adult stem cell studies proved so hard to repeat? One major problem is that the property of "stemness"—the ability of a cell both to renew itself and to give rise to other, more specialised cells—is somewhat elusive. You cannot tell if a cell is a stem cell simply by looking down a microscope. Biologists usually identify stem cells by using antibodies that bind to proteins found on their surfaces, but this can yield ambiguous results. In some cases, teams that cannot repeat one another's results might not even be working with the same cells.

Tracking the fate of stem cells after they are injected into a lab animal is even more difficult. If, say, they turn into heart muscle cells, they will look exactly like any other heart muscle cells. One solution is to add genes to the stem cells that make them fluoresce, but unlabelled cells can fluoresce of their own accord, particularly when damaged. All it takes is a little tweaking with a microscope's controls, or playing with a digital image on a computer, and a dim fluorescent signal can seem as clear as day.

Another method is to replace one of the bases in the stem cells' DNA with a molecule called BrdU. Fluorescent antibodies that bind to BrdU should then reveal the cells' location. Verfaillie, however, has found a serious shortcoming with this technique: if cells die, they can release their BrdU, which may then be taken up by other cells in the vicinity.

Healthy Skepticism Fell by the Wayside

So perhaps it is not surprising that stem cell biologists often disagree about what they are seeing in their microscopes. Yet as excitement mounted about the versatility of adult stem cells, the healthy scepticism that would normally prevail seemed to fall by the wayside. "The scientific standards for publication appeared to get lower and lower as the magnitude of the claims made by those papers got higher and higher," says Sean Morrison, a stem cell researcher at the University of Michigan in Ann Arbor.

Numbers Matter

What's more, the issue is not just whether some adult stem cells can turn into this or that tissue type. It is how many of them do so, something that few papers on adult stem cell plasticity attempt to quantify. Too much has been made of results that are unlikely to be of any medical significance, Keller says.

In some cases, it has turned out that transplanted adult stem cells do not actually give rise to new tissues at all, but instead fuse with cells that are already there. Cell fusion might itself be useful for treating some diseases. But had the phenomenon been recognised earlier on, those in the field might not have got so carried away with the potential of adult stem cells to cure all manner of ills.

Embryonic Stem Cell Results Just as Dubious

Many researchers are just as sceptical about much of the work on human ESCs, which is fraught with many of the same difficulties. For now, however, the biggest questions about ESCs relate to what is going on in culture dishes, rather than in experimental animals.

If ESCs are injected directly into animals, they can form tumours called teratomas. So unlike adult stem cells, ESCs would have to be turned into the specific cell type required before transplantation into people.

For instance, Hans Keirstead of the University of California, Irvine, has got human ESCs to start turning into the precursors of nerve support cells called oligodendrocytes, which in animal experiments seem to repair damaged nerve cells, boosting recovery if injected a week after a spinal injury (but

not 10 months after). On the basis of his work, stem cell company Geron of Menlo Park, California, is planning a clinical trial.

"Black Magic"

Geron would not be considering trials unless it was convinced that Keirstead's team can reliably transform ESCs into oligodendrocyte precursors. The same cannot be said of many other groups. The scientific literature is filled with recipes for turning human ESCs into this or that kind of cell by adding various signalling molecules. Most are little more than "black magic", Keller says.

For starters, many researchers grow their ESCs in a fluid called fetal calf serum, which contains a cocktail of signalling molecules and varies in composition from batch to batch. There is also little quantification of how many cells in a culture adopt a particular fate.

Su-Chung Zhang of the University of Wisconsin–Madison, who has spent several years developing reliable techniques to turn ESCs into neurons, thinks there is an even more fundamental problem. He claims that many cultures that are supposed to contain ESCs have begun to develop into other cell types even before experiments begin. "The vast majority of them are not stem cells," he says. If he is right, much of this research is meaningless.

Researchers and Journals Should Share Blame

In part, stem cell researchers only have themselves to blame for the state their field is in. They reviewed the papers that are now being questioned, and in most cases recommended publication. "What we didn't do is review the papers critically enough," Keller admits. Others argue that the journals, which jostled to publish the hottest papers, must share the blame.

Whoever is at fault, there is now a consensus that tougher standards are needed. Leading stem cell scientists hope that we have seen the end of extravagant claims based on a single line of evidence. "If the phenomenon is real, almost any way you look at it, the same answer will come out," Weissman points out.

Even if stem cell biologists do manage to inject new rigour into their field, outside the laboratory the war of words looks set to continue. Anti-ESC campaigners are already taking advantage of the Korean scandal. "To win public support and government funding ESC advocates have long made hyped claims and exaggerated promises," wrote a campaigner for the US Conference of Catholic Bishops, Richard Doerflinger, in the Catholic publication *Tidings Online*. "In short, they acted like political hucksters instead of scientists, and now are beginning to pay the price."

Such attacks are being met with a vigorous response. "Many of the same critics decrying the overhyping of embryonic stem cell research are the same ones touting equally extravagant claims involving adult stem cells," Shaywitz says. Indeed, Doerflinger has repeatedly promoted contentious claims about the clinical value of adult stem cells.

With the US Senate due to debate various bills on stem cells and cloning, we can expect further claims that stretch the evidence. An end to the hype? Don't believe it.

| "For certain diseases such as juvenile diabetes, embryonic stem cells hold the most promise."

Embryonic Stem Cell Research Is Necessary to Find a Diabetes Cure

Robert Goldstein

In the following viewpoint, Robert Goldstein is testifying before a U.S. Senate subcommittee that embryonic stem cell research offers the most hope of a cure for juvenile diabetes. Goldstein asserts that a cure for this devastating disease is urgently needed to alleviate the suffering and spare the lives of diabetics across the nation. According to Goldstein, scientists around the world believe that embryonic stem cells, not adult stem cells, offer the greatest hope to provide lifesaving therapies for diabetes in the least amount of time. Robert Goldstein is the chief scientific officer of the Juvenile Diabetes Research Foundation, an organization striving to find a cure for diabetes and a leading charitable funder of diabetes research.

Robert Goldstein, testimony before the Senate Commerce Committee Subcommittee on Science, Technology, and Space, July 14, 2004. www.jdrf.org. Reproduced by permission.

As you read, consider the following questions:

1. According to Goldstein, do the "funding commitments" of the Juvenile Diabetes Research Foundation in fiscal year 2004 support their premise that embryonic stem cells offer the greatest hope for a cure to diabetes?

2. How do transplanted pancreatic islet cells ease or even reverse the symptoms of diabetes, according to the author?

3. According to Goldstein, diabetes is the leading cause of which two medical conditions in the United States?

Chairman Brownback and members of this Subcommittee, thank you for the opportunity to appear before you today to participate in this important hearing on adult stem cell research. I am Robert Goldstein, Chief Scientific Officer of the Juvenile Diabetes Research Foundation (JDRF). I am joined today by the Langbein family, who represent the millions of families who struggle with the daily challenges and fears of caring for a loved one with juvenile diabetes. Jamie was diagnosed at the age of one, and she has been on an insulin pump since the age of four. Jamie's diabetes affects her life every day, all day. Her parents must test her blood sugar eight times a day, and every time she eats, exercises, or goes to a birthday party, Jamie must account for what she eats or how much exercise she does and adjust her dose of insulin accordingly so she doesn't end up in the hospital or in a coma. Her mom gave up her career as an attorney so that she could always be nearby if Jamie had problems with her pump or blood sugar while at school, and her parents get up frequently during the night to check her blood sugar level. Jamie worries about being different from her friends in school, and her parents worry about the long-term complications of diabetes and their daughter's future and whether their other children will be diagnosed with the disease. This is just one child of the nearly two million people who battle juvenile diabetes each and every day.

Prevalence of Diabetes

Total: 20.8 million children and adults—7.0% of the population—have diabetes.

    Diagnosed: 14.6 million people

    Undiagnosed: 6.2 million people

    Pre-diabetes: 54 million people

    1.5 million new cases of diabetes were diagnosed in people aged 20 years or older in 2005.

Total Prevalence of Diabetes

Under 20 years of age: 176,500, or 0.22% of all people in this age group have diabetes. About one in every 400 to 600 children and adolescents has type 1 diabetes.

    Two (2) million adolescents (or 1 in 6 overweight adolescents) aged 12–19 have pre-diabetes.

    Although type 2 diabetes can occur in youth, the nationally representative data that would be needed to monitor diabetes trends in youth by type are not available. Clinically-based reports and regional studies suggest that type 2 diabetes, although still rare, is being diagnosed more frequently in children and adolescents, particularly in American Indians, African Americans, and Hispanic/Latino Americans.

    Age 20 years or older: 20.6 million, or 9.6% of all people in this age group have diabetes.

    Age 60 years or older: 10.3 million, or 20.9% of all people in this age group have diabetes.

American Diabetes Association. www.diabetes.org.

Curing Diabetes

JDRF is the leading charitable funder of juvenile diabetes research worldwide. Established more than 30 years ago by parents of children with juvenile diabetes, our mission is to find a cure for juvenile diabetes and its complications. Over the years, JDRF has provided some $800 million in grants for diabetes research at most of the world's leading universities, laboratories, and hospitals. To fund that science, JDRF volunteers do their part every day to raise money in our communities across the country—through walks, galas, and other events—and we are proud of the strong partnership for funding research that we have developed with the federal government.

JDRF, as the world's leading charitable funder of diabetes research, aggressively pursues all avenues of promising research and makes its funding decisions based upon vigorous scientific review based, in many ways, upon the NIH [National Institutes of Health] model. In the area of stem cell science, JDRF funds scientists exploring the opportunities created by both adult and embryonic stem cell research. In Fiscal Year 2004, JDRF commitments in the area of stem cell research total $8.2 million. Of this amount, $6.3 million is spent in the area of embryonic stem cell research and less than $2 million is spent on other areas of stem cell research, including adult stem cells. We focus on both areas—as well as dozens of other avenues of scientific investigation—because no one can predict what area of research will produce new therapies or a cure for juvenile diabetes.

Pancreatic Islet Cell Transplantation

Adult stem cell research has been pursued for more than 35 years, and as you know, embryonic stem cells were just discovered in 1998. JDRF will continue to support both adult and embryonic stem cell research so that we can pursue a cure as strongly as possible. However, the research community believes that embryonic stem cells offer more promise in the area of diabetes. Let me explain why, using pancreatic islet cell transplantation as an example. Islet transplantation has been a spectacular breakthrough in diabetes research. In islet transplantation, the beta—or insulin-producing—cells are isolated from a cadaver pancreas and then infused into a person with juvenile diabetes through a catheter inserted into the portal vein of their liver. Once transplanted, these new islets recognize blood sugar levels and begin to produce and release insulin into the patient's body. Islet transplantation had been attempted since the 1970s with limited success. However, in the year 2000, researchers made a breakthrough in the procedure, and since that time nearly 300 people have received islet transplants and the majority of them lead significantly better and healthier lives. In most of these individuals, therapeutic control of their diabetes has improved remarkably, and in many instances they do not even have to take insulin injections. Furthermore, many of the patients have reported a reversal in some of their complications, especially hypoglycemia [low blood sugar] unawareness but also improvement in vision and less pain from neuropathy [nerve disease].

These results are very exciting, but there are significant hurdles in moving this from an experimental procedure to a standard therapy that could benefit the millions of people with diabetes—many of them children. One such hurdle is the severe shortage of donated pancreases. In 2001, approximately 400 pancreata were available for islet transplantation and research, compared to the almost two million Americans with juvenile diabetes.

Embryonic Stem Cells Give Greatest Hope

Here, then, is one reason why we are so excited about recent advances in embryonic stem cell research. Recent studies have demonstrated the ability to coax embryonic stem cells into insulin-producing cells in the lab. We have good reason to believe that embryonic stem cells will one day be able to grow large amounts of insulin-producing beta cells for transplant, but more work needs to be done. Unfortunately, adult stem cells have not shown the same promise when it comes to diabetes. [In June 2004], Harvard University researcher Douglas Melton published a paper in *Nature* pointing out that in mice, new beta cells in the pancreas are formed through the replication of existing beta cells rather than through the differentiation of adult stem cells. This finding indicates that adult stem cells in the pancreas do not contribute to beta cell formation, and that embryonic stem cells may prove to be the only stem cells that will be useful to generate beta cells for the treatment of Type 1 diabetes. Other studies indicate that mouse embryonic stem cells can be differentiated into insulin-producing cells, and several studies suggest that this can be done using human embryonic stem cells.

JDRF funds research to develop beta cells from adult stem cells, or to regenerate beta cells from existing precursor cells. Researchers have reported that human adult duct tissue might have the potential to develop into beta cells. Other groups have results that indicate that transplanted bone marrow cells may be able to show insulin production. Some have used these findings to argue that adult stem cells may be the answer for curing juvenile diabetes. JDRF takes the position that research using both embryonic and adult stem cells, perhaps even in side-by-side comparisons, will get us to our goal fastest.

Adult stem cells may one day prove to be the answer to alleviating the pain and suffering caused by certain diseases—I certainly hope that is the case. We have heard some remarkable stories from some of the witnesses today. But we have no idea of knowing which diseases those may be, and unfortunately we are not certain of the widespread application of these treatments. We do know that to date, adult stem cells have not been shown to hold as much promise for juvenile diabetes as embryonic stem cells. Given this reality, how can we turn our backs on other exciting research opportunities, such as embryonic stem cell research, thereby potentially delaying life-saving therapies and cures for millions of people? And how can we adequately compare the effectiveness of adult and embryonic stem cell research unless both avenues are pursued simultaneously and with equal rigor?

We are in an extraordinary time of opportunity in the area of medical research, and this country is leading the way. Scientists around the world agree that stem cell research holds tremendous promise for hundreds of millions of people. I applaud you for continuing to monitor advances in the area of adult stem cell research, and I encourage you to do the same for embryonic stem cell research. For certain diseases such as juvenile diabetes, embryonic stem cells hold the most promise, and we can't afford to lose any more time.

No Time to Wait

While we have made great strides towards our goal of a cure, more needs to be done, and we don't have time to wait. Insulin is not a cure for juvenile diabetes, nor does it prevent the onset of complications such as kidney failure, blindness, heart disease and amputations. Diabetic retinopathy is the leading cause of adult blindness in the United States; ninety percent of patients have evidence of retinopathy after fifteen years of diabetes with approximately 25,000 new cases of blindness per year. Diabetes is also the leading cause of renal failure in the United States, accounting for forty percent of new cases per year. Greater than half of all patients with diabetes develop neuropathy, making diabetic neuropathy the most common cause of non-traumatic amputations and autonomic failure. In his or her lifetime, a diabetic patient with neuropathy has a fifteen percent chance to undergo one or more amputations. In the battle against diabetes, we are in a race against time.

Not a day goes by that JDRF doesn't receive calls or letters or email messages from mothers or fathers of children with Type 1 diabetes asking, "When will my child be cured?" On the one hand, it is extremely difficult to explain the pace of science, particularly to a mother whose five-year-old has to prick his finger six or seven times a day to test his blood sugar, who needs three or four injections of insulin every day, who is afraid to go to sleepovers or summer camp for fear of falling into a coma, and who is at constant risk of developing a host of complications that could cut short his life. But on the other hand, it is downright tragic to have to explain how the pace of science could be slowed even further by focusing on one area of research and excluding another.

To put the urgency of finding a cure into perspective, I'd like to share some words from Mary Tyler Moore, JDRF's International Chairman, that she shared with Members of the House. Mary states that "in the nearly six years since human embryonic stem cells were first successfully cultured in a lab, . . . diabetes has contributed to the deaths of as many as 3 million people and cost our nation over $750 billion. It has caused nearly 500,000 amputations, rendered over 100,000 people blind, and forced a quarter million people to require kidney transplants or dialysis. And 120,000 moms have been told that their child has Type 1 diabetes—a disease which during that time period would require each of these children to have 8,700 injections of insulin and 17,500 pricks of their fingers to check blood sugar levels—just for that child to survive."

"Scientists will . . . have to reconsider many claims for embryonic stem cells as a cure for diabetes."

Nonembryonic Stem Cell Research Can Find a Diabetes Cure

Dave Andrusko

In the following viewpoint, Dave Andrusko presents the case for a potential new cure for diabetes that doesn't involve embryonic stem cells. Andrusko argues that the research, which is based on neutralizing the errant white blood cells that cause diabetes, challenges the assumptions of many scientists that embryonic stem cells offer the greatest hope of a cure for diabetes. Dave Andrusko is the editor of the National Right to Life News, *a publication founded in the 1970s to fight abortion. The publishers also oppose euthanasia, human cloning, and human embryonic stem cell research.*

As you read, consider the following questions:

1. According to Andrusko, why is Lee Iacocca's foundation raising money to cure diabetes?

Dave Andrusko, "Diabetes in Mice Cured Using Non-Embryonic Sources," *National Right to Life News*, 2005. www.nrlc.org/news. Reproduced by permission.

2. What is the current source of most transplanted islet cells, according to the author?

3. According to Michael Fumento, as cited by Andrusko, what are two possible reactions to implanted embryonic stem cells?

To most Americans, the enduring image of Lee Iacocca is of the charismatic head of the Chrysler Corporation during the 1980s. His role as philanthropist is much less well known.

Iacocca's wife, Mary, died of complications from Type I diabetes [in 1984]. Following her death, as Iacocca has said many times, "my family and I began a journey to support innovative diabetes research."

Questioning Conventional Wisdom

Iacocca's foundation is currently raising $11 million to support the work of Dr. Denise Faustman, whose research team in 2003 not only reversed, but actually cured Type I diabetes in mice. This is of particular interest to pro-lifers because her work is proving yet again that there is no need to lethally scavenge stem cells from human embryos to treat diseases.

To get a good feel for Dr. Faustman's work, ironically, you could hardly do better than this quote from (of all places) the November 9, 2004, edition of the *New York Times*. Writes Gina Kolata, "Dr. Faustman's story, scientists say, illustrates the difficulties that creative scientists can have when their work questions conventional wisdom and runs into entrenched interests. But if she is correct, scientists will also have to reconsider many claims for embryonic stem cells as a cure for diabetes, and perhaps for other diseases."

At first glance, you wouldn't think that finding additional financing that builds on a genuine medical first would be hard. But it has been excruciatingly difficult.

Kolata says that Dr. Faustman and some colleagues believe the reason is simple: "her findings, which raise the possibility

Requirements for Curing Diabetes

It is generally believed that an effective cure for type 1 diabetes will require two substantial scientific advances. First, in order to restore the pancreas' ability to produce insulin, new islet beta cells must be provided, either by transplanting cells from a healthy donor or by encouraging the growth and/or function of the diabetic patient's own cells. Second, to protect the new beta cells, no matter what their origin, it is necessary to repair the breakdown in immunological tolerance that precipitated the anti-islet attack in the first place.

Diabetes Monitor, March 23, 2006.
www.diabetesmonitor.com.

that an inexpensive, readily available drug might effectively treat Type 1, or juvenile diabetes, challenge widespread assumptions." Among the assumptions, held by "many diabetes researchers" is the insistence that "a cure lies . . . in research on stem cells and islet cell transplants."

Dr. Faustman, an associate professor of medicine at Harvard, thinks otherwise.

Islet Cell Transplants

Insulin is produced by clusters of cells in the pancreas called the islets of Langerhans. Insulin, a hormone, helps the body use glucose (sugar) for energy.

Diabetes results when a white blood cell mistakes islet cells for foreign tissue. As a key component of the body's immune system, the misguided white cell then does its duty: it multiplies and destroys the islets.

Until recently most research trying to treat Type I diabetes assumed the patient would receive an islet cells transplant to replace those killed by the marauding white blood cells. Most of those islet cells came from cadavers.

Caught up in the frenzy over the supposed unlimited curative powers of embryonic stem cells, many have begun to argue that harvesting islet cells from cadavers is inefficient and unnecessary. They contend that the best technique is to harvest embryonic stem cells which, they theorize, could be altered into becoming islet cells. This is part and parcel of the hype that embryonic stem cells can be changed into any body cell as easy as pie and without danger to the patient.

Ethical Solution

Dr. Faustman, an associate professor of medicine at Harvard, has moved in a much more productive and ethically unobjectionable direction. Working with colleagues at the diabetes unit at Massachusetts General Hospital, she discovered that they could neutralize the attacking white cells "by supplying them with a piece of protein that signaled that the islet cells were normal cells," Kolata writes.

But what about the white cells already laying siege to the pancreas? These white cells need to be destroyed.

According to Kolata, one of Dr. Faustman's breakthroughs was to give mice a very, very inexpensive off-patent drug that stimulates the release of an immune system hormone which kills the offending white cells. However, the real eye-opener was what followed the administration of both treatments to mice.

Not only did the immune system's attack on the islet cells cease, the islets grew back! At the time, this was completely unheard of.

The obvious question was, where were the new cells coming from? The "surprising answer" was the spleen.

What did Dr. Faustman's work show? That targeted disease removal was sufficient, without the need for cells from any external source. The once diabetic animals regenerated islets from cell precursors that already existed in their bodies. Ironically, while there has been a major emphasis on identifying cells for transplantation to treat Type I diabetes, there had been no prior evidence that self-healing was not possible through regeneration.

Embryonic Stem Cells: Wrong Solution

Consider how this research both neutralizes the case for embryonic stem cells and points out its multiple weaknesses.

As mentioned, a number of researchers say the answer is to just program embryonic stem cells to become islet cells and avoid the difficult and time-consuming task of harvesting islet cells from cadavers. However, this "solution" is wrong on three grounds.

First, it hasn't been demonstrated to work. Second, as science writer Michael Fumento has observed, not only do embryonic stem cells "implanted into animals have a nasty tendency to cause malignant tumors," the "body rejects them just as it rejects donated organs." Moreover, unless the underlying disease is cured, new cells—regardless of source—would be destroyed.

But as the magazine *Diabetes Health* wrote in its January 2005 edition, "If the [body's] capacity to regenerate can be harnessed to replenish insulin-producing islet cells that are destroyed by disease, then perhaps a 'transplant' of stem cells or islets may not be needed."

The Iacocca Foundation is raising $11 million to fund the initial phase of a clinical trial in humans based on Dr. Faustman's success in mice. According to the February *Diabetes Health*, there are two primary emphases.

Dr. David Nathan is a colleague of Dr. Faustman at Massachusetts General. He'll be investigating whether the immune system hormone (BCG) used in mice will kill the islet-killing white blood cells, and, if it does, examine "safety, optimal timing for administration and best dosage," according to the February *Diabetes Health*.

Dr. Faustman will be "working on a blood test that will immediately assess the effects of BCG by determining whether the dangerous white cells are being destroyed," Kolata writes.

As for Iacocca, he is eager to push on—and now. "I can't wait for the pharmaceutical companies or even government tax money to fund what looks promising," Iacocca told Kolata. "They are not known for high risk and they are also slow to react. We are trying to get a cure."

"Reports that stem-cell therapy for Alzheimer's will never work are somewhat exaggerated."

Embryonic Stem Cell Research May One Day Cure Alzheimer's Disease

Sharon Begley

The potential for embryonic stem cells to cure Alzheimer's disease, a haunting affliction that takes away a person's memories and sense of who they are, is the focus of the following viewpoint by Sharon Begley. Begley acknowledges that Alzheimer's is an extremely complex brain disease and other more straightforward brain diseases may be better candidates for stem cell cures. But, she contends, even though it may take longer to find a stem cell cure for Alzheimer's than to find one for Parkinson's disease or Huntington's disease, striking research results on neurons indicate that it is definitely possible. Begley, a former writer for Newsweek, *is a science writer for the* Wall Street Journal.

As you read, consider the following questions:

1. According to the author, how many types of neurons die in Parkinson's disease?

2. What reason does Begley use to suggest that the challenge to cure Alzheimer's will be greater than that of curing Parkinson's, Huntington's, or spinal cord injuries?

3. According to Jeffrey Macklis, as cited by the author, how many years might it take to find a stem cell cure for Alzheimer's?

Now that news cycles seem to be measured in mere minutes, I'd swear that backlashes are coming before lashes.

In Round 1, proponents of embryonic stem-cell research seized on [former First Lady] Nancy Reagan's May 8 [2004] speech supporting such experiments and piggy-backed on her husband's death from Alzheimer's disease to urge President [George W.] Bush to lift the crippling restrictions he placed on stem-cell studies.

Opponents immediately fired back. Citing a *Washington Post* article that called Alzheimer's "among the least likely to benefit" from stem-cell therapy, pro-life Web sites and periodicals accused scientists and "abortion scammers" of trying to pull a fast one.

To paraphrase Mark Twain, reports that stem-cell therapy for Alzheimer's will never work are somewhat exaggerated.

Neural Repair No Longer Considered Absurd

In the early 1990s, "the idea that you could achieve cellular repair of the highest-level, most complex neural circuitry," like that ravaged by Alzheimer's, "was widely considered absurd," says neuroscientist Jeffrey Macklis of Harvard Medical School, Boston. But after a decade of discoveries, especially the finding that the adult brain contains "precursor cells" able to morph into neurons, "we're seeing that what people thought was impossible—to get new neurons wired into existing circuitry—isn't."

Not that it will be easy. Even in brain diseases way less complex than Alzheimer's, results have been underwhelming.

In Parkinson's Disease, for instance, only one kind of neuron (making the neurotransmitter dopamine) in only one part of the brain dies. You'd think that would be straightforward to fix. Indeed, when scientists took mouse embryonic stem cells, coaxed them to bloom into dopamine-making neurons, and transplanted them into the brains of rats suffering from a Parkinson's-like disease, the rats' motor function improved. But in other such studies the cells either disappeared or reverted to an essentially useless type, notes Eugene Redmond, who directs neural transplantation at Yale University.

Human studies have also been disappointing. In Parkinson's, some patients have improved after receiving fetal (not embryonic) cells; others got worse. The story is much the same in Huntington's disease and spinal-cord injury.

Daunting, but Not Impossible

In Alzheimer's, the challenge is greater. Entire circuits underlying memory and thought, in many regions of the brain, are wiped out. Expecting transplanted neurons to weave themselves into the fraying circuits seems about as likely as a skein of yarn inserting itself into a damaged tapestry and re-creating the original. As Dr. Redmond says, "getting new cells to make the proper connections is daunting."

But maybe not impossible. In one tantalizing study, neuroscientist Kiminobu Sugaya of the University of Central Florida, Orlando, transplanted about 10,000 human neural stem cells from fetuses into the brains of memory-impaired rats, whose age of 24 months corresponds to a human age of about 80. After the transplant, most of the once-forgetful rats could navigate a water maze, a test of memory, as adeptly as rats one-fourth their age.

Even more strikingly, microscopic examination showed that the stem cells had not only differentiated into neurons. They had also "become incorporated into brain areas related to spatial memory," says Prof. Sugaya.

The key, he believes, was injecting the stem cells into the region of the mouse brain from which its own neural stem cells surge out and migrate to their targets. Maybe damaged neurons send out an SOS, attracting replacement cells. If so, then transplanted cells may also receive the SOS and find the target.

That seems to explain Prof. Macklis's success, too. When he induced the death of neurons in complex circuits in mouse brains, mimicking Alzheimer's, he found that the "synaptic partners" of the dying neurons acted like abandoned lovers: They started calling for new partners.

Specifically, the now-partnerless neurons emitted signals that coaxed precursor cells in the mice's brains to become newly minted neurons. About half of the new neurons migrated to the site of cell death, Dr. Macklis and colleagues found. Most made the same receptors and neurotransmitters as the lost neurons; many hooked up with the neurons that had called to them.

"It is now feasible to think about incorporating new neurons into the adult brain," says Dr. Macklis. "Though it will be difficult, I think we as a field will be able to rebuild neural circuits." For simple circuits, such as those severed in spinal-cord injury, that may happen within 10 years. Repairing the complex circuits of Alzheimer's may take 30.

Which cells will make the best "neuroreplacements"? Those from embryonic stem cells, which are so ethically fraught? Or the brain's own precursor cells, which sit in a sort of reservoir, waiting to morph into neurons and enter the fray?

"We are years away from using the brain's precursor cells therapeutically," says neurologist Mark Mehler of New York's Albert Einstein College of Medicine. "In the meantime, we should use anything we have, including embryonic stem cells."

The obstacles are formidable. All the more reason to throw everything we can at these diseases.

> *"Of all the diseases that may someday be cured by embryonic stem cell treatments, Alzheimer's is among the least likely to benefit."*

Embryonic Stem Cell Research Is Unlikely to Cure Alzheimer's Disease

Rick Weiss

In the following viewpoint, Rick Weiss argues that the chances of embryonic stem cell treatments curing Alzheimer's disease are remote. According to Weiss, advocacy groups spurred to action by Nancy Reagan after former U.S. president Ronald Reagan's death from the devastating disease are touting immediate embryonic stem cell cures for Alzheimer's. Most scientists, however, think Alzheimer's is too complex to be cured by embryonic stem cell treatments, contends Weiss. Rick Weiss is a science and medical reporter for the Washington Post.

As you read, consider the following questions:

1. According to Weiss, why did President Bush say he placed limits on the field of stem cell research?

2. Why is Alzheimer's disease, in contrast to Parkinson's disease and spinal cord injuries, not likely to be "cured" by embryonic stem cells, in the author's opinion?

3. Short of a cure, how, according to Weiss, could embryonic stem cell research help to find the cause of Alzheimer's?

Ronald Reagan's death from Alzheimer's disease on June 5, 2004, has triggered an outpouring of support for human embryonic stem cell research. Building on comments made by [his widow] Nancy Reagan . . . , scores of [U.S.] senators . . . called upon President [George W.] Bush to loosen his restrictions on the controversial research, which requires the destruction of human embryos. Patient groups have also chimed in, and Senate Majority Leader Bill Frist . . . added his support for a policy review.

It is the kind of advocacy that researchers have craved for years, and none wants to slow its momentum.

Embryonic Stem Cells Not a Likely Cure

But the infrequently voiced reality, stem cell experts confess, is that, of all the diseases that may someday be cured by embryonic stem cell treatments, Alzheimer's is among the least likely to benefit.

"I think the chance of doing repairs to Alzheimer's brains by putting in stem cells is small," said stem cell researcher Michael Shelanski, co-director of the Taub Institute for Research on Alzheimer's Disease and the Aging Brain at the Columbia University Medical Center in New York, echoing many other experts. "I personally think we're going to get other therapies for Alzheimer's a lot sooner."

Stem cell transplants show great potential for other diseases such as Parkinson's and diabetes, scientists said. Someday, embryo cell studies may lead to insights into Alzheimer's.

If nothing else, some said, stem cells bearing the genetic hall-marks of Alzheimer's may help scientists assess the potential usefulness of new drugs.

Public Distortion

But given the lack of any serious suggestion that stem cells themselves have practical potential to treat Alzheimer's, the Reagan-inspired tidal wave of enthusiasm stands as an example of how easily a modest line of scientific inquiry can grow in the public mind to mythological proportions.

It is a distortion that some admit is not being aggressively corrected by scientists.

"To start with, people need a fairy tale," said Ronald D.G. McKay, a stem cell researcher at the National Institute of Neurological Disorders and Stroke. "Maybe that's unfair, but they need a story line that's relatively simple to understand."

Promising for *Some* Diseases

Human embryonic stem cells have the capacity to morph into virtually any kind of tissue, leading many scientists to believe they could serve as a "universal patch" for injured organs. Some studies have suggested, for example, that stem cells injected into an injured heart can spur the development of healthy new heart muscle.

Among the more promising targets of such "cellular therapies" are: Parkinson's disease, which affects a small and specialized population of brain cells; type-1 diabetes, caused by the loss of discrete insulin-producing cells in the pancreas; and spinal cord injuries in which a few crucial nerve cells die, such as the injury that paralyzed actor Christopher Reeve.

In part as a result of her friendship with Hollywood personalities Doug Wick, Lucy Fisher, and Jerry and Janet Zucker—all of whom have become stem cell activists because they have children with diabetes—Nancy Reagan became interested in stem cells and their oft-cited, if largely theoretical,

Stem Cell Research Is Not a Priority

The Alzheimer's Association's goal is to eradicate Alzheimer's through the advancement of research. We therefore support any legitimate scientific avenue that offers the potential to advance this goal within appropriate boundaries. That said, human stem cell research is not a current research priority for the Alzheimer's Association. Promising areas of Alzheimer's disease research today include:

- Understanding the role of amyloid in the brain.

- Risk factors related to genetics and lifestyle.

- Risk factors related to cardiovascular disease and metabolic disorders.

- Therapies to slow or stop the progression of the disease.

- Brain imaging for early diagnosis and improving drug testing.

*"The Alzheimer's Association Statement Regarding
Human Stem Cell Research," June 2004. www.alz.org*

potential for treating Alzheimer's. Over the years, she has become more vocal on the issue.

On May 8, [2004,] with her husband's brain ravaged by Alzheimer's disease, Nancy Reagan addressed a biomedical research fundraiser in Los Angeles and spoke out forcefully.

"I just don't see how we can turn our backs on this," she said, in an oblique cut at Bush, who placed tight limits on the field in August 2001 to protect, he said, the earliest stages of life.

Since Reagan's death, many others have joined the call to enlist embryonic stem cells in the war on Alzheimer's, including some new converts. Among the 58 senators who signed the letter to Bush were 14 Republicans and several abortion opponents—evidence that the Reagan connection is providing "political cover," said Sean Tipton of the Coalition for the Advancement of Medical Research, a stem cell advocacy group.

Alzheimer's Is Too Complex

But in contrast to Parkinson's, diabetes and spinal injuries, Alzheimer's disease involves the loss of huge numbers and varieties of the brain's 100 billion nerve cells—and countless connections, or synapses, among them.

"The complex architecture of the brain, the fact that it's a diffuse disease with neuronal loss in numerous places and with synaptic loss, all this is a problem" for any strategy involving cell replacement, said Huntington Potter, a brain researcher at the University of South Florida in Tampa and chief executive of the Johnnie B. Byrd Institute for Alzheimer's Research.

"We don't even know what are the best cells to replace initially," added Lawrence S.B. Goldstein, who studies stem cells and Alzheimer's disease at the University of California at San Diego. "It's complicated."

Goldstein and others emphasized that future Alzheimer's patients could benefit if stem cell research is allowed to blossom.

Some Studies Could Help

Scientists suspect, for example, that stem cell studies could help identify the molecular errors that underlie Alzheimer's, which in turn would help chemists design drugs to slow or even reverse the disease.

But that line of work could face formidable political hurdles. That is because the most frequently cited approach would require not just stem cells from spare embryos donated by fertility clinics—a currently untapped source of cells that many want Bush to make available to federally funded researchers. It would also require the creation of cloned human embryos made from cells taken from Alzheimer's patients.

From such embryos, stem cells bearing the still-unidentified defects underlying Alzheimer's could be removed and coaxed to grow into brain cells in lab dishes, and their development could be compared to the development of normal brain cells.

While that experiment could shed important light on the earliest—and perhaps most treatable—stages of Alzheimer's, a majority in Congress have said that the creation of cloned human embryos is an ethical line they are unwilling to cross.

Less controversial uses of stem cells may also lead to insights, Goldstein and others said. The key, said Harvard stem cell researcher George Daley, is not to get "preoccupied with stem cells as cellular therapies." Their real value for Alzheimer's will be as laboratory tools to explore basic questions of biology, Daley said.

Immediate Cures Unlikely

Unfortunately, said James Battey, who directs stem cell research for the National Institutes of Health, "that is not necessarily the way I hear the disease community talking. They tend to focus on the immediate use of stem cells for their disease or disorder."

It is not clear whether the recent wave of stem cell support will persist as it becomes clearer that cures remain far off—and, in the case of Alzheimer's, unlikely. Basic research with stem cells is just as deserving of support as therapeutic trials, Battey said, "but it's a much harder sell."

"The public should understand that science is not like making widgets," he said. "We're exploring the unknown, and by definition we don't know where it's going to take us."

Periodical Bibliography

The following articles have been selected to supplement the diverse views presented in this chapter.

Carolyn Abraham	"A Sobering Setback in Stem Cell Research," *Toronto Globe and Mail*, October 23, 2006.
Michael Clarke and Michael W. Becker	"Stem Cells: The Real Culprits in Cancer?" *Scientific American*, July 2006.
Jon Cohen	"Stem Cell Pioneers," *Smithsonian*, December 2005.
Clive Cookson et al.	"The Future of Stem Cells," *Scientific American*, July 2005.
Martin Enserink	"Selling the Stem Cell Dream," *Science*, July 14, 2006.
Stephanie Horvath	"Family Pins Hopes for Son on Stem-Cell Shots," *Palm Beach* (FL) *Post*, June 19, 2005.
Jonathan Kimmelman, Françoise Baylis, and Kathleen Cranley Glass	"Stem Cell Trials: Lessons from Gene Transfer Research," *Hastings Center Report*, January/February 2006.
National Institutes Of Health	*Regenerative Medicine*, 2006. http://stemcells.nih.gov/.
National Institutes Of Health	"Stem Cell Basics," *Stem Cell Information*, 2006. http://stemcells.nih.gov/.
Helen Philips	"Stem Cell Trial to Combat Childhood Brain Disease," *New Scientist*, September 2006.
David A. Prentice	"Current Science of Regenerative Medicine with Stem Cells," *Journal of Investigative Medicine*, January 2006.
Rick Weiss	"The Power to Divide," *National Geographic*, July 2005.

OPPOSING
VIEWPOINTS®
SERIES

CHAPTER 2

What Ethical and Moral Questions Surround Stem Cell Research?

Chapter Preface

If embryonic stem cells are used to replace injured or diseased cells in patients, as many people envision, large numbers of donated oocytes (egg cells) will be necessary to create cloned embryonic stem cells genetically matched to patients. In the cloning procedure, called somatic cell nuclear transfer (SCNT), the nucleus of an oocyte is removed and replaced with the nucleus of an adult somatic (body tissue) cell. The procedure is not very efficient. For each successful cloning event there are usually hundreds of failed attempts. Disgraced South Korean stem cell researcher, Woo-Suk Hwang, who falsely claimed to have been the first to clone a human embryo and extract stem cells from it, reportedly amassed thousands of eggs over a three year period and used hundreds in his research—and he was still unsuccessful. The methods Hwang used to obtain these eggs have put egg donation in the spotlight, especially the issue of compensating women for their eggs. Many people believe that it is unethical to pay women who donate egg cells for stem cell research, while others consider it unethical not to pay them.

The process of egg cell donation is time-consuming, uncomfortable and even painful, requires surgery, and carries a multitude of risks, complications, and side effects. Physicians use needle extraction to retrieve anywhere from a few to a couple of dozen oocytes from anesthetized donors during a brief surgical procedure. Before the procedure, donors receive daily hormone injections for a week to ten days, which overstimulates the ovaries to produce more than the usual single oocyte per menstrual cycle. The American Society for Reproductive Medicine estimates that egg donors spend fifty-six hours undergoing interviews, counseling, and medical procedures related to the process. As women's health advocate Judy Norsigian writes, "The drugs used to hyperstimulate the ovaries also have negative effects, most notably a condition called Ovarian Hyperstimulation Syndrome (OHSS). Serious cases of this syndrome involve the development of cysts and enlargement of the ovaries, along with massive fluid build-up in the body." Some women have even died from OHSS.

Those who oppose compensating women for their eggs, writes Emily Galpern, of the Center for Genetics and Society in Oakland, California, maintain that "compensation creates a financial incentive for economically vulnerable women to expose themselves to both known and unknown health risks for money. A market in eggs for research would emerge, valuing women's reproductive tissue over their well-being." But others argue that because of the time, discomfort, and risk involved it is unethical not to pay women for stem cell research egg donation. They also contend that other donors of tissue are routinely paid. Men who donate sperm, women who donate their eggs to help other couples conceive, and many clinical research participants are usually compensated for their donations. Writes Josephine Johnson of the Hastings Center, "Many research subjects in the United States also receive compensation in exchange for enrollment in clinical trials or other investigations. Proponents of this practice argue that such payment, particularly where modest, is not only a necessary incentive but also fair treatment of research subjects." Advocates of egg donation payment believe that without financial incentives there just won't be enough egg donors to supply the multitude of eggs necessary for stem cell research.

The ethics of egg donation are being debated at the national and international level as scientists and bioethicists anticipate the future needs of stem cell research. Whether or not women should be compensated for egg donation is one of many ethical issues related to stem cell research. The contributors of the viewpoints in the following chapter explore other ethical and moral questions related to stem cell research.

| "Sacrificing human embryos would fundamentally depart from the long-honored Hippocratic ethic which teaches, 'First, do no harm.'"

Destroying Embryos in Order to Obtain Stem Cells Is Immoral

William Cheshire

In the following viewpoint, William P. Cheshire Jr. argues that early embryos are nascent human life and as such they warrant respect, awe, and protection. Cheshire says embryos are more than mere clumps of cells. From the very first moment of conception, he says, embryos have profound intrinsic worth, and destroying them for embryonic stem cell research is immoral and unethical. Cheshire warns that if we lose our respect and sense of awe for the earliest moments of developing human life, we devalue the basic good of all human life. Cheshire is a professor of neurology at the Mayo Clinic in Jacksonville, Florida.

William Cheshire, "Letter to President's Bioethics Council," Christian Medical and Dental Associations, April 15, 2003. www.cmawashington.org. Reproduced by permission.

As you read, consider the following questions:

1. What reason does Cheshire give for some of his patients' rejection of the benefits of embryonic stem cell research?

2. As reported by the author, what do the Nuremberg Code and the Declaration of Helsinki prohibit?

3. According to Cheshire, when do some bioethicists say that a developing human life gains moral relevance?

In this [viewpoint] I will offer the view that policies governing the experimental treatment of human embryos ought to respect the dignity of nascent human life. In support of this assertion I will appeal to the sense of awe that naturally arises in response to the evidence of neuroscience, which in its analysis of human life points to innate value that transcends physical description.

I am a clinical neurologist at an academic medical center and have been practicing medicine for 16 years. I think it appropriate to mention that I have no direct financial interest in the development or regulation of biotechnology or any personal research agenda to protect that might influence my judgment on these issues. Rather, I am writing out of a sense of moral obligation as a physician.

Perhaps some of you might wonder why a neurologist would be concerned about embryonic biotechnology, since the human embryo does not yet possess a nervous system. In answering that question, I would like to suggest that, when considering how embryonic biomedical research touches human lives, the limited perspective of the embryologist is incomplete. Not all that is of value in the life of the human embryo can be glimpsed through the lens of the microscope focused on cellular structure. The true significance of new human life must be inferred by appreciating the fullness of its connection with humanity. This connection includes the embryo's real (not abstract) potential to develop and actualize the remarkable capabilities associated with the human brain.

Embryo Destruction Is Unethical

Each day I care for patients with neurodegenerative diseases, including, for example, Parkinson's disease, Alzheimer's disease, and multiple system atrophy. Many of them could be eligible for some of the treatments predicted one day [to] result from advances in stem cell technology. I share my patients' hopes for new and better treatments through science. I am also sensitive to the trust that my patients place in the medical profession to choose ethically, when it comes to the personal care they receive, and when it comes to the moral direction in which we choose to guide biomedical research.

The concern so many of my patients have shared with me relates to the prospect of generating human embryos for purposes other than procreation. For many of them such a prospect is unconscionable. Whether the means of creating embryos is through in vitro fertilization or cloning via somatic cell nuclear transfer, and whether the purpose of creating them is to increase options for preimplantation genetic selection or to harvest embryonic stem cells, in each case what is proposed is creating new human lives and then causing their death. Although it is plainly true that these human embryos would be destroyed at a very early stage in their development, it is also plainly true that the lives destroyed are human lives. Some of my patients have indicated that they would reject the benefits of such technology out of deeply held moral convictions.

Hippocratic Oath

Regardless of their personal choice whether to partake of particular biotechnologies, many of my patients recognize that acquiescing to a research program relying on the destruction of human embryos would, in any case, represent an historical shift in the conduct of biomedical science. In particular, sacrificing human embryos would fundamentally depart from the long-honored Hippocratic ethic which teaches, "First, do no harm." Most seem to perceive this at an intuitive level, like the little girl in the [Norman] Rockwell painting who tests her doctor's ethical behavior by seeing how he will treat her rag doll. The doctor wins her confidence by first placing his stethoscope to the chest of the doll and listening tenderly. In art as in medicine, it matters to patients how their physicians treat others. To illustrate how much biotechnology is altering the tones of the American medical canvas, imagine this: The child in the painting must now ask whether her doctor would be willing to dissect her embryo sister to engineer a treatment for her disease.

Public conscience has time and again reaffirmed the Hippocratic ethic in such statements as the Nuremberg Code and the Declaration of Helsinki, which preclude conscripting human beings for lethal research without their informed consent. It is important to note that these ethical codes do not exempt human beings at the beginning of life as not falling under the protection that ought to be due all human subjects, especially the young and vulnerable. When deciding how to treat the human embryo, in wisdom we should pause to consider how history will judge our age if we remove protection from a segment of humanity by assigning them ambiguous moral worth. At stake in this decision is, I believe, the integrity of the medical profession, which should always regard highly the value of human life.

Embryos Are Much More than Cells

As a physician it is my view that every human life, from the first moment of existence, has profound intrinsic worth that should be protected. As a neurologist my understanding of the human nervous system buttresses this view. The human brain,

Determining the Beginning of Moral Status

Central to many of the bioethical issues of our time is the question When should society confer moral status on an embryo? When should we call an embryo or a fetus one of us? The fertilized egg represents the starting point for the soon-to-be dividing entity that will grow into a fetus and finally into a baby. It is a given that a fertilized egg is the beginning of the life of an individual. It is also a given that it is not the beginning of *life*, since both the egg and the sperm, prior to uniting, represent life just as any living plant or creature represents life. Yet is it right to attribute the same moral status to that human embryo that one attributes to a newborn baby or, for that matter, to any living human? Bioethicists continue to wrestle with the question. The implications of determining the beginning of moral status are far-reaching, affecting abortion, in vitro fertilization, biomedical cloning, and stem cell research. The rational world is waiting for resolution of this debate.

Michael S. Gazzaniga, The Ethical Brain, 2005.

indubitably, is the most complex and elegantly designed structure in the known universe. Its ten billion integrated neurons with a hundred trillion interconnections far surpass the capabilities of the world's most sophisticated computers, not only in degree but also in category of function. A mere three pounds of tissue demonstrates remarkable skills for learning symbolic language, abstract reasoning sufficient to discuss ethics, and motor coordination delicate enough that a trained musician can perform a Bach violin sonata. Furthermore, the human mind possesses distinct capacities outside the range of quantitative measurement and which continue to defy, and lie somewhere beyond, precise scientific explanation, including consciousness, awareness of personal identity over time, free will, the striving for purpose, for hope, willingness to self-sacrifice, and concern for moral responsibility. These phenomena impress me as being reliable evidence that the human organism is not just a chemical machine, but is a being whose essential nature is in part mysterious.

Some will overlook the human embryo as an entity quite small and thus apparently trivial. Attempts, however, to establish meaning solely by counting the number of cells involved leads to absurd conclusions. Modern neuroimaging techniques have shown, for example, that experiences such as listening to music, recognizing human faces, and expression of language are associated with increased metabolic activity in certain well-localized regions of the brain. Spoken speech may light up a single gyrus [brain ridge]. Would we deem a child's smile at recognizing his mother, or the anguish of mourning, to be relatively unimportant if their corresponding brain processes consisted only of collections of cells shifting their patterns of electrolyte conductance? Of course not. To collapse the meaning of such experiences in proportion to the small numbers of recruited neurons associated with mental awareness and comprehension would be as cynical as to claim that a single human being is unimportant in comparison to the size of the Earth or the Solar System. On independent grounds we recognize life experiences to mean much more than can be described simply by the flux of neurotransmitters among scattered clusters of cells.

Biological or physical attributes, while important, fail to explain all we know to be true of human beings and thus are inadequate criteria for the purpose of assessing not only meaning but also moral status. Just as the mind is more than the molecules of the brain, the human being is more than the sum of its matter, and the human embryo much more than so many cells. Human life has unique dignity [that] science cannot measure. At all points along the continuum of the human life span, the worth of humanity lies beyond the field of view of strictly empirical investigation. Likewise, the methods of the embryologist are incompetent to disprove the assertion that the human embryo possesses special human dignity.

Moral Relevance

While some bioethicists prefer to acknowledge moral relevance only in beings who satisfy a specified threshold of cognitive function, that approach misses the deeper truth. The more fundamental question is what kind of a being possesses the capacity for assembling within itself a structure as wondrous as the human brain? The human embryo is such a being—the same kind of being as you and I—regardless of whether she has yet actualized all her latent capacities. The human organism at every stage of development is the type of being that, if provided basic care and nurture, possesses the potential for amazing neurological accomplishment.

That a being capable of learning, love, and laughter, of sonnets, science, and space exploration begins the life journey within the humble edifice of a zygote [a single-celled human embryo] transcends comprehension. That the magnificent human brain unfolds from a genetic blueprint compactly arranged within a single cell marking the beginning of human life arouses inexpressible awe. We dare not evaluate the human embryo apart from this due sense of awe. Such awe is not diminished by the small size of the embryo, but rather is all the greater when we appreciate the capabilities just emerging within the nascent human individual. The tiny embryo is the living link joining one generation to another, and in this new life reaching afresh into the world resides the full potential of our human future.

More important than the laudable goals of scientific knowledge and technological gain is the basic good of human life itself, through which and for which science exists. It is my view, therefore, that human embryos should be created only for purposes of procreation, and that applications that rely on destroying nascent human life should be prohibited. To permit lethal research on living human embryos would be tantamount to a reversal of moral progress in bioethics. To dismiss the humanity of the embryo for the sake of scientific or economic gain would also move us dangerously closer to setting aside the dignity of other vulnerable classes of humanity.

Consequences

I will conclude by reflecting briefly on the consequences of devaluing the basic good of human life. In the course of ethical deliberation over how to treat the human embryo, we should also consider what kind of people we would become if we were to relinquish our sense of awe and wonder in response to observing early human life. To lose sight of the transcendent value of early human life would be to risk abandoning the inestimable value of human life at all stages of maturation, growth, and decline. A society that allows itself to become indifferent to what is done to human embryos would inevitably coarsen its sensitivity toward other individuals. Indeed, how society decides to treat the least of human lives is a measure of how it chooses to value vulnerable and impaired human beings in general. And who among us is not in some way vulnerable or impaired, or by some standard too young or too old?

> "Embryonic stem cell research is morally
> permissible because, although embryos
> deserve respect, they are not morally
> equivalent to human beings."

Destroying Embryos in Order to Obtain Stem Cells Is Not Immoral

Jonathan D. Moreno and Sam Berger

In the following viewpoint, Jonathan D. Moreno and Sam Berger argue that embryonic stem cell research is moral because embryos have a lesser moral status than human beings. Moreno and Berger are responding to opponents of embryo research, who oppose it for moral reasons and are generally supporters of President George W. Bush's stem cell policy. Moreno and Berger assert that they and other supporters of embryonic stem cell research have considered the ethics and morality of embryo research and have concluded that under appropriate research guidelines it is morally permissible. Jonathan D. Moreno is a senior fellow at the Center for American Progress, an American political policy research and advocacy organization. Sam Berger is the fellows assistant to Moreno and others at the center.

Jonathan D. Moreno and Sam Berger, "Taking Stem Cells Seriously," *The American Journal of Bioethics*, vol. 6(5), 2006. Reproduced by permission of Taylor & Francis Group, LLC. www.taylorandfrancis.com.

As you read, consider the following questions:

1. According to the authors, what is the "pluralistic" approach in the context of embryonic stem cell research?

2. According to the Genetics and Public Policy Center study cited by Moreno and Berger, what percentage of Americans believe that embryos have no moral status?

3. What are examples of ways that embryonic stem cell research can be monitored to ensure that the research is "justified" do the authors give?

Conservative opponents of embryonic stem cell research frequently argue that supporters of the medical research focus on scientific technicalities at the expense of morality. Eric Cohen, editor of the neoconservative journal *The New Atlantis*, puts the complaint succinctly:

> [C]ritics of the [President George W.] Bush policy should also address its supporters on their own terms, and rather than argue only about scientific adequacy, they should consider seriously the moral dilemma the policy seeks to address.

Cohen seems to suggest that the critics of the Bush policy have not addressed the ethical issues surrounding embryonic stem cell research. Yet, as Cohen surely knows, numerous authoritative bodies have explained the moral justifications for the research, and most Americans share these views. Cohen and other conservative bioethicists often appear to regard those who do not share their ethical views as lacking in moral seriousness, a position that is itself unserious in its estimation of those who have legitimate disagreements.

Not an All-or-Nothing Matter

Embryonic stem cell research is morally permissible because, although embryos deserve respect, they are not morally equivalent to human beings. This moral argument was described in the 1994 *Report of the Human Embryo Research Panel* (HERP) for the National Institutes of Health (NIH) as the pluralistic approach: Rather than focus on a single feature to determine when embryos are considered morally equivalent to full persons, the pluralistic approach holds that "protect-ability is not an all-or-nothing matter but results from a being's increasing possession of qualities that make respecting it more compelling" (NIH 1994). As human life develops, it begins to take on added moral worth and gains added respect and rights; arguing that a sperm or a collection of cells in a Petri dish are morally equivalent to a living person, or even a developing fetus, fails to recognize the emergent character of human life and personhood.

The HERP report contrasts this pluralistic approach with attempts to find a single criterion that clearly establishes moral status, such as genetic identity or development potential. These attempts inevitably "create paradoxes in logic and run counter to many widely accepted practices," such as contraception and in vitro fertilization, problems which do not plague the plu-ralistic approach. The pluralistic approach acknowledges that while an embryo does not entail the same legal and moral protections as a person, it is still valued and protected; em-bryo destructive research may be conducted, but it must be "well-justified research."

Consensus on Embryo's Lesser Moral Status

Scientific bodies, presidential advisory councils, philosophers and theologians of all faiths, and the general public all sup-port regulated embryonic stem cell research based on the lesser moral status of the embryo. As the National Bioethics Advisory Commission (NBAC) stated in *Ethical Issues in Hu-man Stem Cell Research,*

> we have found substantial agreement among individuals
> with diverse perspectives that although the human embryo

and fetus deserve respect as forms of human life, the scientific and clinical benefits of stem cell research should not be foregone.

Both the American Association for the Advancement of Science and the National Academy of Science have concluded that respect for human embryos does not prohibit embryonic stem cell research, and no presidential council, including the [George W. Bush] one, has determined that the embryo's moral status precludes research on it.

The American people also support the nuanced view that embryos possess lesser moral status than persons. Recent polls show that anywhere from 57% to 67% of Americans support stem cell research, and the same Genetics and Public Policy Center study that found that 67% of people support the research also determined that only 30% of the respondents believe the embryo has no moral status. Furthermore, the study found that, of those who do accord human embryos the highest moral status, one-third still support human embryonic stem cell research. People do have respect for embryos, which is why they want to ensure that research using them proceeds carefully, ethically and with clear regulations and oversight.

Details Determine Morality

The moral argument of stem cell supporters explains their predilection with scientific technicalities and regulation; the morality of the research depends on these crucial details.

Engaging in the serious moral debate at hand means examining the specifics of research procedures, the current state of technology and potential success rates to ensure the research is justified. Research guidelines like those put forward by the National Academies, which require institutional review boards and oversight committees, help ensure that research is "well-justified" enough to ethically allow the destruction of embryos. Ethical standards for stem cell research will need to change along with technology, scientific knowledge and societal attitudes. To ensure ethics keep pace with these changes, and to maintain transparency and public engagement in embryonic stem cell research policies and practices, the National Academies ha[ve] recently created a committee to monitor the field, updating and adjusting research guidelines as needed.

Serious Introspection

We are confident, however, that opponents of embryonic stem cell research will continue to depreciate such efforts by the scientific community, and therefore the views of most Americans that they reflect, as lacking in moral seriousness. Diversity of opinion is welcome, but assertions that the proponents of embryo research have failed to address the moral issues are simply false. It is time for these critics to engage in the sort of serious introspection they demand of others.

> *"The point is to cause each of us to think deeply about whether there is any essential difference between the reality of [World War II] Nazi experiments and 'therapeutic cloning.'"*

Therapeutic Cloning to Obtain Embryonic Stem Cells Is Immoral

David A. Prentice and William Saunders

In this two-part viewpoint, David A. Prentice and William Saunders discuss the science and the ethics of therapeutic cloning. In the first part, Prentice argues that creating clones for the purpose of embryonic stem cell research, called "therapeutic cloning," is no different from reproductive cloning, which creates a living human child. Also, he points out, therapeutic cloning is not therapeutic for the embryo. In the second part of the viewpoint, Saunders builds on Prentice's argument and goes even further. He argues that therapeutic cloning is really no different than the horrific experiments performed by the Nazis during World War II. Saunders notes that supporters of embryonic stem cell re-

David A. Prentice and William Saunders, from *Human Cloning and the Abuse of Science*. Washington, DC: Family Research Council, 2004. Copyright © 2004 by Family Research Council. All rights reserved. Reproduced by permission of Family Research Council, 801 G Street NW, Washington, DC 20001, 800-225-4008, www.frc.org.

search contend that the research is beneficial to humankind; however, Saunders argues, the Nazis used this same reasoning to justify research on the mentally ill, the disabled, and the feeble-minded. Prentice and Saunders are senior fellows at the Family Research Council, a conservative Christian think tank and lobbying organization.

As you read, consider the following questions:

1. Why does Prentice claim that therapeutic cloning will lead to reproductive cloning?
2. What was the point of the Nuremberg Code, according to Saunders?
3. Why does Saunders say that therapeutic cloning violates the Nuremberg Code?

Part I

Cloning always starts with an embryo. The most common technique proposed for human cloning is called somatic cell nuclear transfer (SCNT). This cloning is accomplished by transferring the nucleus from a human somatic (body) cell into an egg cell which has had its chromosomes removed or inactivated. SCNT produces a human embryo who is virtually genetically identical to an existing or previously existing human being.

Proponents of human cloning hold out two hopes for its use: (1) the creation of children for infertile couples (so-called "reproductive cloning"), and (2) the development of medical miracles to cure diseases by harvesting embryonic stem cells from the cloned embryos of patients (euphemistically termed "therapeutic cloning").

All Human Cloning Produces a Human Being

All human cloning is reproductive. It creates—reproduces—a new, developing human intended to be virtually identical to the cloned subject. Both "reproductive cloning" and "therapeutic cloning" use exactly the same technique to create the clone, and the cloned embryos are indistinguishable. The process, as well as the product, is identical. The clone is created as a new, single-cell embryo and grown in the laboratory for a few days. Then it is either implanted in the womb of a surrogate mother ("reproductive cloning") or destroyed to harvest its embryonic stem cells for experiments ("therapeutic cloning"). It is the same embryo, used for different purposes. In fact, the cloned embryo at that stage of development cannot be distinguished under the microscope from an embryo created by fertilization joining egg and sperm. Trying to call a cloned embryo something other than an embryo is not accurate or scientific. Biologically and genetically speaking, what is created is a human being; its species is *Homo sapiens*. It is neither fish nor fowl, neither monkey nor cow—it is human. . . .

Created in Order to Be Destroyed

"Therapeutic cloning" is obviously not therapeutic for the embryo. The new human is specifically created in order to be destroyed as a source of tissue [, as Robert P. Lanza and colleagues report in a 2000 *JAMA* article]: "[Therapeutic cloning] requires the deliberate creation and disaggregation of a human embryo."

Most cloned embryos do not even survive one week, to the blastocyst stage, when they are destroyed in the process of harvesting their cells. Experiments with lab animals show that even these early embryos have abnormalities in genetic expression. . . .

Beyond the abnormalities caused by the cloning procedure, embryonic stem cells from cloned embryos will still face problems for their use, including the tendency to form tumors, and significant difficulties in getting the cells to form the correct tissue and function normally. . . .

Therapeutic Cloning Leads to Reproductive Cloning

Because there is no difference in the nuclear transfer technique or the cloned embryo, allowing "therapeutic cloning" experimentation to proceed will inevitably lead to "reproductive cloning." The technique can be practiced and huge numbers of cloned embryos produced. In fact, the lead scientist of the South Korean team that first cloned human embryos in February 2004 in a press conference on their experiments that the cloning technique developed in their laboratory "cannot be separated from reproductive cloning." His statement affirms what others have pointed out before: allowing therapeutic cloning simply prepares the way for reproductive cloning.

Human cloning is unsafe and unnecessary. There are no valid or compelling grounds—scientific or medical—to proceed. A comprehensive ban on human cloning is the only sufficient answer.

Part II

As Dr. Prentice has shown, cloning indisputably destroys innocent human life. This basic truth should lead the world to reject human cloning. However, in an effort to extricate human cloning from this ethical vise grip, its supporters attempt to draw a distinction between human life, which begins at conception, and human "personhood," which begins only at their say-so.

Unfortunately, the arbitrary denial of "personhood" to human beings has a long and cruel history. The Nuremberg Code, formulated in the years after World War II, is particularly instructive with regard to the current debate on human cloning. For instance, when the principal author of the report on human cloning issued by the National Academy of Sciences testified before the President's Council on Bioethics, he stated that "reproductive cloning" would violate the Nurem-

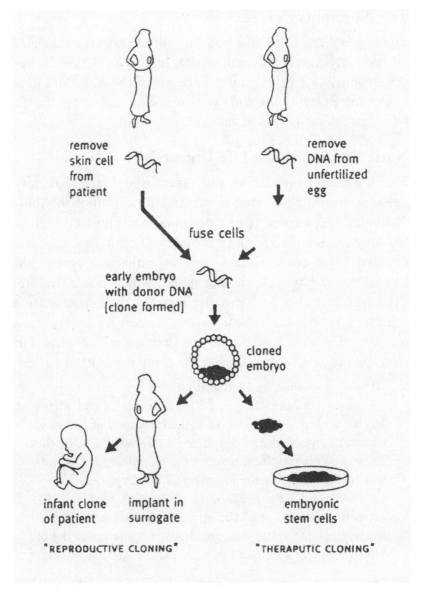

remove
skin cell
from
patient

remove
DNA from
unfertilized
egg

fuse cells

early embryo
with donor DNA
[clone formed]

cloned
embryo

infant clone   implant in
of patient   surrogate

embryonic
stem cells

"REPRODUCTIVE CLONING"   "THERAPUTIC CLONING"

berg Code: "The Nuremberg Code, with which I am in full agreement, outlines those kinds of things you would not simply [do] for the sake of knowledge that involve human subjects."

The Nuremberg Code

The Nuremberg Code is a body of ethical norms enunciated by the Nuremberg Tribunal, which, after World War II, had the responsibility of judging the actions of the Nazis and their allies. The point of the code was to restate and apply the established ethical norms of the civilized world.

Nazis Deemed Some Life Unworthy

Nazi laws had defined Jews and other "undesirables" as non-persons. Eventually, between six and nine million of these "undesirables" were sent to extermination camps and killed. However, before the killing in the camps began, the Nazis had engaged in an extensive campaign of euthanasia against the mentally and physically handicapped, which not only foreshadowed but also prepared the way for the extermination camps. In his book *The Nazi Doctors*, Robert Jay Lifton draws our attention to a book titled *The Permission to Destroy Life Unworthy of Life*, written during the campaign. Lifton writes:

> [It was] published in 1920 and written jointly by two ... German professors: the jurist Karl Binding ... and Alfred Hoche, professor of psychiatry at the University of Freiburg. Carefully argued in the numbered-paragraph form of the traditional philosophical treatise, the book included as "unworthy life" not only the incurably ill but large segments of the mentally ill, the feeble-minded, and retarded and deformed children. . . . [T]he authors professionalized and medicalized the entire concept; destroying life unworthy of life was "purely a healing treatment" and a "healing" work.

The Nazis were determined to "cleanse" the genetic pool to produce "better" Aryans. Nazi officials announced that "under the direction of specialists ... all therapeutic possibilities will be administered according to the latest scientific knowledge." The result of this therapeutic treatment of "inferior" lives was that "eventually a network of some thirty killing areas within existing institutions was set up throughout Germany and in

Austria and Poland." In their book, *The Nazi Doctors and the Nuremberg Code,* George Annas and Michael Grodin reveal that:

> At the same time that forced sterilization and abortion were instituted for individuals of "inferior" genetic stock, sterilization and abortion for healthy German women were declared illegal and punishable (in some cases by death) as a "crime against the German body." As one might imagine, Jews and others deemed racially suspect were exempted from these restrictions. On November 10, 1938, a Luneberg court legalized abortion for Jews. A decree of June 23, 1943, allowed for abortions for Polish workers, but only if they were not judged "racially valuable."

Later, the Nazis created the extermination camps for the Jews and other "inferior" races. In the camps, Nazi doctors engaged in cruel experiments on the Jews, Gypsies, Poles, and others. They exposed them to extreme cold to determine the temperature at which death would occur. They injected them with poisons to see how quickly certain lethal elements moved through the circulatory system. They subjected twins to all manner of disabling and brutal experiments to determine how genetically identical persons reacted to different conditions.

Some of the experiments were nonetheless designed to preserve life—not of the subject, but of, for example, German pilots who were forced to parachute into freezing ocean waters.

Everyone agrees the Nuremberg Code prohibits "reproductive cloning." What relevance does it have for "therapeutic cloning?" If human embryos are human beings, then "therapeutic cloning," which creates an embryo only to destroy it in the process of exploiting its stem cells, violates a cardinal principle of the Nuremberg Code: There is to be no experimentation on a human subject when it is known that death or disabling injury will result. Regardless of the good that might be produced by such experiments, the experiments are of their very nature an immoral use of human beings. . . .

Subverting the Meaning of Healing

Recall how the Nazis subverted the meaning of healing. Recall how they used the term "therapeutic" to describe not the helping of suffering people, but the killing of them. Recall that the Nazis eliminated those "unworthy of life" in order to improve the genetic stock of Germany. Recall how the Nazis undertook lethal experiments on concentration camp inmates in order, in some cases, to find ways to preserve the lives of others.

The point is not to suggest that those who support "therapeutic cloning" are, in any sense, Nazis. Rather, the point is to cause each of us to think deeply about whether there is any essential difference between the reality of those Nazi experiments and "therapeutic cloning." As we have shown, each case involves a living human being, and that human being is killed in the aim of a perceived "higher" good.

Cloning proponents try to distinguish between the two cases by saying that the cloned human being has no "potential." But in each case, it is the actions of other human beings that rob the first of "potential" (in the first case, the actions of Nazi executioners; in the second, the laboratory technicians). In either case, the human subject is full of potential simply by being a living human being. Of course, almost miraculously, many of the inmates of the camps did survive when the allies rescued them. Equally miraculously, frozen embryos have been implanted in a woman's womb and brought to live (and healthy) birth.

As we have shown, every embryo is not merely "potentially" a life, but [is an] actual life, a human being from the first moment of existence. Furthermore, any living human embryo has the inherent "potential" to develop into a healthy baby. It is disingenuous for supporters of cloning to claim the cloned human embryo is only "potential life" because they plan to mandate by law that it be destroyed before it can come to birth. Regardless of its location, the human embryo, by its nature, is full of potential, unless the actions of adult human beings deprive it of the opportunity to realize that potential.

Guard Against Inhuman Acts

[Russian author] Alexander Solzhenitsyn, a man who chronicled and suffered under another ideology that denied the dignity of each and every human being, observed, "Gradually it was disclosed to me that the line separating good and evil passes not through states, nor between classes, nor between political parties either, but right though every human heart, and through all human hearts. This line shifts. Inside us, it oscillates."

Solzhenitsyn did not regard the perpetrators of brutal crimes in his own country as inhuman monsters. Rather, he saw the essential truth—they were human beings, engaged in immoral acts. They engaged in those acts by dehumanizing the persons on whom their brutality was inflicted, and they did so in the name of (perhaps in the passionate belief in) a greater good. But Solzhenitsyn reminds us that, unless we are willing to admit that, for the best as well as for the worst of motives, we are also capable of inhuman acts, we will have no guard against committing them. No one is safe from brutality so long as we think that it is only inhuman others who are capable of inhuman acts. Rather, we will be secure when we are willing to look honestly at the objective reality of our acts, while realizing that we, too, are capable of acts that violate the inherent dignity of another, and refuse to engage in such acts despite the good we believe would result from doing otherwise. In the debate over the cloning and destruction of embryonic human beings, this essential truth must be our guide.

> "Stem cell research to cure debilitating disease . . . is a noble exercise of our human ingenuity to promote healing."

Therapeutic Cloning to Obtain Embryonic Stem Cells Is Not Immoral

Michael J. Sandel

In the following viewpoint, Michael J. Sandel argues that cloning an embryo in order to extract its stem cells, called therapeutic cloning or biomedical cloning, is not immoral. First, he argues that cloned embryos are really no different than embryos produced through in vitro fertilization (IVF). Then he argues that extracting stem cells from either cloned embryos or IVF embryos is not immoral because an embryo does not have the same moral status as a living human being. Sandel contends that therapeutic cloning should be allowed to proceed subject to regulations that respect the nascent human life. Michael J. Sandel is a political philosopher and professor of government at Harvard University.

As you read, consider the following questions:

1. What questions does Sandel say must be confronted in order to decide the ethical implications of cloning?

Michael J. Sandel, "The Ethical Implications of Human Cloning," *Perspectives in Biology and Medicine*, vol. 4, spring 2005, pp. 241–47. Copyright © 2005 The Johns Hopkins University Press. Reproduced by permission.

2. Does the author think it is okay to extract stem cells from spare embryos left over at fertility clinics?

3. How does Sandel describe the "equal moral status" view?

In this [viewpoint], I will consider the ethics of reproductive and therapeutic cloning. But I want also to advance a more general claim: that the cloning issue, and related debates about genetic engineering, will change the way philosophers think about their subject. Much of the debate about cloning and genetic engineering is conducted in the familiar language of autonomy, consent, and individual rights. Defenders of "liberal eugenics" argue that parents should be free to enhance the genetic traits of their children for the sake of improving their life prospects. Ronald Dworkin, for example argues that there is nothing wrong with the ambition "to make the lives of future generations of human beings longer and more full of talent and hence achievement." In fact, he maintains, the principle of ethical individualism makes such efforts obligatory. Many opponents of cloning and genetic engineering also invoke the language of autonomy and rights. . . .

But talk of autonomy and rights does not address the deepest questions posed by cloning. In order to grapple with the ethical implications of cloning, we need to confront questions largely lost from view in the modern world—questions about the moral status of nature and about the proper stance of human beings toward the given world. Since questions such as these verge on theology, or at least involve a certain view of the best way for human beings to live their lives, modern philosophers and political theorists tend to shrink from them. But our new powers of biotechnology make these questions unavoidable.

In the United States today, no federal law prohibits human cloning, either for purposes of reproduction or for purposes of biomedical research. This is not because most people favor reproductive cloning. To the contrary, public opinion and almost all elected officials oppose it. But there is strong disagreement about whether to permit cloning for biomedical research. And the opponents of cloning for biomedical research have so far been unwilling to support a separate ban on reproductive cloning, as Britain has enacted. Because of this stalemate, no federal ban on cloning has been enacted. . . .

The Ethics of Cloning for Biomedical Research

I turn now to the ethics of cloning for biomedical research. It is here that the greatest disagreement prevails. The U.S. Senate is split between those who want to ban all cloning and those who want to ban reproductive cloning but not cloning for stem cell research and regenerative medicine. . . . As in the case of reproductive cloning, the concepts of autonomy and rights cannot by themselves resolve the moral question. In order to assess the moral permissibility of cloning for stem cell research, we need to determine the moral status of the early embryo. If the six-day[-old], pre-implantation embryo ([called a] blastocyst) is morally equivalent to a person, then it is wrong to extract stem cells from it, even for the sake of curing devastating diseases such as Parkinson's, Alzheimer's, or diabetes. If the embryo is a person, then not only should all therapeutic cloning be banned, so also should all embryonic stem cell research.

Cloned and Spare IVF Embryos: No Distinction

Before turning to the moral status of the embryo, I would like to consider one influential argument against cloning for biomedical research that stops short of opposing embryonic stem cell research as such. Some opponents of research cloning, troubled by the deliberate creation of embryos for research, support embryonic stem cell research, provided it uses "spare" embryos left over from fertility clinics. Since in vitro fertilization (IVF) clinics (at least in the United States) create many more fertilized eggs than are ultimately implanted, some argue that there is nothing wrong with using those spares for research: if excess embryos would be discarded anyway, why not use them (with donor consent) for potentially life-saving research?

This seems to be a sensible distinction. But on closer examination, it does not hold up. The distinction fails because it begs the question whether the "spare" embryos should be created in the first place. If it is immoral to create and sacrifice embryos for the sake of curing or treating devastating diseases, why isn't it also objectionable to create and discard spare IVF embryos in the course of treating infertility? Or, to look at the argument from the opposite end, if the creation and sacrifice of embryos in IVF is morally acceptable, why isn't the creation and sacrifice of embryos for stem cell research also acceptable? After all, both practices serve worthy ends, and curing diseases such as Parkinson's, is at least as important as enabling infertile couples to have genetically related children.

Of course, bioethics is not only about ends, but also about means. Those who oppose creating embryos for research argue that doing so is exploitative and fails to accord embryos the respect they are due. But the same argument could be made against fertility treatments that create excess embryos bound for destruction. In fact, a recent study found that some 400,000 frozen embryos are languishing in American fertility clinics, with another 52,000 in the United Kingdom and 71,000 in Australia.

If my argument is correct, it shows only that stem cell research on IVF spares and on embryos created for research (whether natural or cloned) are morally on a par. This conclusion can be accepted by people who hold very different views about the moral status of the embryo. If cloning for

Stem Cells, Not Babies

Somatic Cell Nuclear Transfer (a.k.a. "therapeutic cloning") is about saving and improving lives. It is fundamentally different from human reproductive cloning; SCNT produces stem cells, not babies.

- In Somatic Cell Nuclear Transfer (SCNT), the nucleus of a donor's unfertilized egg is removed and replaced with the nucleus of a patient's own cells, like a skin, heart, or nerve cell. These types of cells are called somatic cells.

- The goal of SCNT is to develop stem cells that will not be rejected or destroyed by the patient's immune system.

- No sperm is used in this procedure.

- The cells are not transplanted into a womb.

- The unfertilized egg cells are stored in a petri dish to become a source of stem cells that can be used to treat life-threatening medical conditions.

- SCNT aims to treat or cure patients by creating tailor-made, genetically identical cells that their bodies won't reject. In other words, SCNT could allow patients to be cured using their own DNA.

Coalition for Advancement of Medical Research.
stemcellfunding.org.

stem cell research violates the respect the embryo is due, then so does stem cell research on IVF spares, and so does any version of IVF that creates and discards excess embryos. If, morally speaking, these practices stand or fall together, it remains to ask whether they stand or fall. And that depends on the moral status of the embryo.

The Moral Status of the Embryo

There are three possible ways of conceiving the moral status of the embryo: as a thing, as a person, or as something in between. To regard an embryo as a mere thing, open to any use we may desire or devise, is, it seems to me, to miss its significance as nascent human life. One need not regard an embryo as a full human person in order to believe that it is due a certain respect. Personhood is not the only warrant for respect: we consider it a failure of respect when a thoughtless hiker carves his initials in an ancient sequoia, not because we regard the sequoia as a person, but because we consider it a natural wonder worthy of appreciation and awe—modes of regard inconsistent with treating it as a billboard or defacing it for the sake of petty vanity. To respect the old growth forest does not mean that no tree may ever be felled or harvested for human purposes. Respecting the forest may be consistent with using it. But the purposes should be weighty and appropriate to the wondrous nature of the thing.

Difficulties with "Equal Moral Status" View

One way to oppose a degrading, objectifying stance toward nascent human life is to attribute full personhood to the embryo. I will call this the "equal moral status" view. One way of assessing this view is to play out its full implications, in order to assess their plausibility. Consider the following hypothetical: a fire breaks out in a fertility clinic, and you have time to save either a five-year-old girl or a tray of 10 embryos. Would it be wrong to save the girl?

A further implication of the equal moral status view is that harvesting stem cells from a six-day-old blastocyst is as morally abhorrent as harvesting organs from a baby. But is it? If so, the penalty provided in the proposed U.S. anti-cloning legislation—a $1 million fine and 10 years in prison—is woefully inadequate. If embryonic stem cell research is morally equivalent to yanking organs from babies, it should be treated as a grisly form of murder, and the scientist who performs it should face life imprisonment or the death penalty.

A further source of difficulty for the equal moral status view lies in the fact that, in natural pregnancies, at least half of all embryos either fail to implant or are otherwise lost. It might be replied that a high rate of infant mortality does not justify infanticide. But the way we respond to the natural loss of embryos or even early miscarriages suggests that we do not regard these events as the moral or religious equivalent of infant mortality. Otherwise, wouldn't we carry out the same burial rituals for the loss of an embryo that we observe for the death of a child?

The conviction that the embryo is a person derives support not only from certain religious doctrines but also from the Kantian assumption [made by philosopher Immanuel Kant] that the moral universe is divided in binary terms: everything is either a person, worthy of respect, or a thing, open to use. But this dualism is overdrawn.

The way to combat the instrumentalizing impulse of modern technology and commerce is not to insist on an all-or-nothing ethic of respect for persons that consigns the rest of life to a utilitarian calculus. Such an ethic risks turning every moral question into a battle over the bounds of personhood. We would do better to cultivate a more expansive appreciation of life as a gift that commands our reverence and restricts our use. Human cloning to create designer babies is the ultimate expression of the hubris that marks the loss of reverence for life as a gift. But stem cell research to cure debilitating disease, using six-day-old blastocysts, cloned or uncloned, is a noble exercise of our human ingenuity to promote healing and to play our part in repairing the given world.

Therapeutic Cloning Should Be Allowed

Those who warn of slippery slopes, embryo farms, and the commodification of ova [egg cells] and zygotes [fertilized eggs] are right to worry but wrong to assume that cloning for biomedical research necessarily opens us to these dangers. Rather than ban stem cell cloning and other forms of embryo research, we should allow it to proceed subject to regulations that embody the moral restraint appropriate to the mystery of the first stirrings of human life. Such regulations should include licensing requirements for embryo research projects and fertility clinics, restrictions on the commodification of eggs and sperm, and measures to prevent proprietary interests from monopolizing access to stem cell lines. This approach, it seems to me, offers the best hope of avoiding the wanton use of nascent human life and making these biomedical advances a blessing for health rather than an episode in the erosion of our human sensibilities.

"Biotechnology [such as stem cell research] threatens the very basis of human morality as we know it."

Stem Cell Treatments Threaten Human Morality

Paul Lauritzen

In the following viewpoint, Paul Lauritzen presents a moral argument against stem cell research that doesn't hinge upon the moral status of a days-old embryo. Most moral arguments against embryonic stem cell research are based on the view that the embryo is a human life and should not be destroyed even to extract stem cells, while adult stem cell research is considered acceptable because it does not involve embryo destruction. Lauritzen challenges this notion, however. He argues that the actual moral problem with stem cell research has to do with treatments that significantly lengthen the human life span or create human-nonhuman species, which are a cross between humans and animals. These activities, says Lauritzen, threaten the very basis of human morality. Paul Lauritzen is a professor of theology and religious studies at John Carroll University in Cleveland, Ohio.

Paul Lauritzen, "Stem Cells, Biotechnology, and Human Rights," *The Hastings Center Report*, vol. 35, March–April 2005, pp. 25–33. Copyright © 2005 Hastings Center. Reproduced by permission.

As you read, consider the following questions:

1. What does Lauritzen say are the two broad concerns posed by stem cell research?

2. As cited by the author, what does ethicist Gilbert Meilaender say forms the basis of human attitudes toward death and dying?

3. What are some of the possible negative consequences of a significant increase in the average length of the human life span, according to Lauritzen?

> ... the final stage is come when man by eugenics, by prenatal conditioning, and by an education and propaganda based on perfect applied psychology, has obtained full control over himself. Human nature will be the last part of nature to surrender to man. —C. S. Lewis, *The Abolition of Man*

> This sudden shift from a belief in Nurture, in the form of social conditioning, to Nature, in the form of genetics and brain physiology is the great intellectual event, to borrow Nietzsche's term, of the late twentieth century. —Tom Wolfe, *Hooking Up*

I begin with passages from this unlikely pair of authors because, although they represent somewhat different times, differ in temperament, and differ extravagantly in personal style, they share an imaginative capacity to envision the possible consequences of modern technology. The technology that occasioned Lewis's reflections—"the aeroplane, the wireless, and the contraceptive"—may now seem quaint, but the warning he sounded about turning humans into artifacts was eerily prescient. Similarly, although he does not directly take up stem cell research, Tom Wolfe's reflections on brain imaging technology, neuropharmacology, and genomics are worth noting in relation to the future of stem cell research. In his inimitable way, Wolfe summarizes one view of the implications of this technology in the title of the essay from which the above passage comes. "Sorry," he says, "but your soul just died."

A Debate over More than Embryo Status

The point of beginning with Lewis and Wolfe is not that I share their dire predictions about the fate to which they believe technology propels us; instead, I begin with these writers because they invite us to take an expansive view of technology. I believe that a broader perspective is needed in the ongoing public debate over stem cell research and that such a perspective is in fact beginning to emerge. This is not to say that the traditional analysis that has framed much of the debate—analysis of autonomy, informed consent, and commodification, for example—is unhelpful; far from it. Nevertheless, much of the debate about stem cell research has focused on the enormously divisive issue of embryo status. Indeed, the debate about stem cell research seems almost choreographed, the steps all too familiar from the dance of abortion politics. The upshot is that much of the stem cell debate has been too narrowly focused and is repetitive and rigid. For that reason, I urge that we consider stem cell research together with other forms of biogenetic research and therapy. Among other things, shifting the frame of reference in this way would require us to attend much more carefully to issues raised by adult stem cell work. Thus, instead of beginning with a question about embryo status, let us start with a question that has not typically been asked: Is adult stem cell work as unproblematic as it is often assumed to be?

[Director of the National Human Genome Research Institute] Francis Collins's testimony before the President's Council on Bioethics in December 2002 suggests why this may be a productive question. Collins was asked to speak about "genetic enhancements: current and future prospects," and what he said about pre-implantation genetic screening [PGD] is instructive. He noted that we are now able to screen both gametes [reproductive cells] (sperm or egg) and embryos, but because gamete screening is currently limited to sorting sperm for sex selection, he did not discuss it at length. He did, however, offer an interesting observation. Focusing on gametes, he says, is useful because it "isolates you away from some of the other compelling arguments about moral status of the embryo and allows a sort of cleaner discussion about what are the social goods or evils associated with broad alterations in the sex ratio and inequities in access to that technology." In other words, the ethical issues raised by pre-implantation genetic screening are not limited to those brought about by the destruction of embryos required by PGD; indeed, screening gametes also raises serious moral issues, ones that might be eclipsed if we focus exclusively on embryos.

Embryonic *and* Adult Stem Cells Raise Moral Concerns

Might we not make a similar claim about embryonic and adult stem cell research? Adult stem cell research is often thought to sidestep some of the issues raised by work on embryonic stem cells, but in fact, does it not raise many of the most pressing issues surrounding embryonic stem cell research, only in a somewhat cleaner and more direct form?

I believe it does, and that we need to attend to a whole range of issues related to embodiment, species boundaries, and human nature that are raised by recent developments in what [bioethicist] Bruce Jennings has referred to as the "regime of biopower." I will discuss two broad concerns posed by stem cell research and related biotechnological interventions. The first has to do with the prospect of transforming the contours of human life in fairly dramatic ways. The second has to do with our attitudes toward the natural world. As we move to change the meaning of human embodiment in fundamental ways, including the possibility of eroding species boundaries, we need to ask whether we are prepared to reduce the entire natural world to the status of an artifact. These concerns raise questions about the meaning of human rights in a posthuman future.

The Natural Trajectory of Human Life

To get a sense of what kinds of issues arise when we consider changing the contours of human existence, consider the notion that there is a species-typical pattern for human life that gives a determinate shape to our lives, a shape that has normative significance. On this view, there is a natural "trajectory" to human life, a natural ebb and flow from conception to death, that has implications for developing moral and political positions across a range of social issues, from reproductive technology to physician-assisted suicide. Yet stem cell research appears to challenge the idea of a natural trajectory to human life.

For example, [medical sociologists] Catherine Waldby and Susan Squier argue that the derivation of stem cells from early embryos demonstrates that embryos do not have one developmental trajectory. According to Waldby and Squier, stem cell research reveals the plasticity of early embryonic material, and in doing so demonstrates "the perfect contingency of any relationship between embryo and person, [and] the non-teleological [no end purpose] nature of the embryo's developmental pathways." Indeed, they say, this research shows "that the embryo's life is not proto-human, and that the biology and biography of human life cannot be read backwards into its moments of origin." This claim may at first appear to be about embryo status, but Waldby and Squier mean to imply much more. In effect, they reject the notion that there is a meaningful trajectory to human life. What was killed when stem cells were first derived from the inner cell mass of a blastocyst, they say, was not a person, but a "biographical idea of

The Biotechnological Promise

By the end of this century, the typical [person] may attend a family reunion in which five generations are playing together. Great-great-great grandma, at 150 years old, will be as vital, with muscle tone as firm and supple, skin as elastic and glowing, as her 30-year-old great-great-granddaughter with whom she's playing tennis.

After the game, while enjoying a plate of vegetables filled with not only a solid day's worth of nutrients but medicines she needs to repair damage to her ageing cells, she'll be able to chat about some academic discipline she studied in the 1980s with as much acuity and memory as her 50-year-old great-grandson, who is studying it now....

This idyll is more than realistic, given reasonably expected breakthroughs and extensions of our knowledge of human, plant and animal biology, as well as mastery of the manipulation of these biologies to meet our needs and desires.

Ronald Bailey, April 11, 2006. www.reason.com.

human life, where the narrative arc that describes identity across time has been extended to include the earliest moments of ontogeny [beginning of being]."

That much more is at stake here than whether embryos are persons is clear if we attend to those who subscribe to the notion of a trajectory of a human life. [Ethicist] Gilbert Meilaender, for example, has argued that our attitudes toward death and dying are shaped by our conception of what it means to have a life. Indeed, according to Meilaender, two views of what it means to have a life and to be a person have been at war with each other over the past thirty years, and these views underwrite sharply different positions on practically every bioethical issue. On Meilaender's view, having a life means precisely that one is following a trajectory that traces a "natural pattern" that "moves through youth and adulthood toward old age and, finally, decline and death." As he puts it, "to have a life is to be terra animata, a living body whose natural history has a trajectory." Although Meilaender develops the notion of a natural trajectory primarily to address the issue of euthanasia, not stem cell research, talk of "natural history," "natural pattern," and "natural trajectory" is also relevant to stem cell research and related technologies. These new biotechnologies might fundamentally change our views about how and even whether a human life is constrained by the natural aging process. The question these biotechnologies raise, then, is whether such a change should be resisted.

Altering the Human Life Cycle

There is little doubt that Meilaender would resist significant alteration of the natural trajectory, and other members of the President's Council on Bioethics, prominently Leon Kass and Francis Fukuyama, have raised similar concerns. But while those who oppose biotechnological interventions that may change the shape of the human life cycle are sometimes lumped together as "life cycle traditionalists," it is important to note that changing the trajectory of a life raises two distinct concerns.

The first is a more or less straightforward concern about the social consequences of altering the human life cycle. This concern is nicely illustrated by Francis Fukuyama's discussion of the social implications of dramatically lengthening the human life span in his book *Our Posthuman Future*. Suppose, he says, that regenerative medicine realizes its promise and the average life span expands from seventy to 110 years or more. What social dislocations can we expect? To explore this question, Fukuyama divides an aging cohort into two categories: the first category comprises people age sixty-five up to eighty-five; the second category is age eighty-five and older. The consequences of greatly expanding membership in these categories should give us pause, Fukuyama concludes, even if older people are much more vigorous than they are today. "For virtually all of human history up to the present," he writes,

> people's lives and identities were bound up either with reproduction—that is, having families and raising children—or with earning the resources to support themselves and their families. Family and work both enmesh individuals in a web of social obligations over which they frequently have little control and which are a source of struggle and anxiety, but also of tremendous satisfaction. Learning to meet those social obligations is a source of both morality and character.
>
> People in Categories I and II, by contrast, will have a much more attenuated relationship to both family and work. They will be beyond reproductive years, with links primarily to ancestors and descendants. Some in Category I may choose to work, but the obligation to work and the kinds of mandatory social ties that work engenders will be replaced largely by a host of elective occupations. Those in Category II will not reproduce, not work, and indeed will see a flow of resources and obligations moving one way: toward them.

Other possible negative consequences include a growing burden on the environment due to overpopulation, a prolongation of adolescent immaturity, increased burdens on an already strained health care system, and other social costs.

What It Means to Be Human

The second concern is often expressed in terms of a threat to human identity or what it means to be human, and although this concern frequently has a consequentialist cast, it comes in a largely non-consequentialist form as well. [Ethicist] Walter Glannon has developed the most interesting form of the identity argument. According to Glannon, one direct consequence of significantly increasing the human lifespan would be to attenuate the relationship among past, present, and future mental states of a self and thus undermine the psychological grounds of personal identity. Since a sense of psychological connectedness between the present and the future is necessary to ground future-oriented desires, the inevitable erosion of a sense of connectedness that would come with a much longer life would, paradoxically, result in the extinction of the desire for a longer life. Without a reasonably strong sense of psychological connectedness to some future self, one would have little reason to take an interest in the potential projects of that person.

In Glannon's formulation, there would be biological continuity between a present and distant future self, but psychological discontinuity: "there would be a divergence of our biology from our psychology." Strictly speaking, it would be more accurate (and also more helpful) to say that a new biology would result in a new psychology. And, in fact, such a formulation is more consistent with Glannon's analysis, one aspect of which involves examining the formation-storage-retrieval process by which the brain maintains the equilibrium between remembering and forgetting that is critical to psychological unity. Discussing the function of activator and blocker CREB (cyclic AMP response element binary protein), Glannon writes:

> The function of this protein suggests that the requisite unity between these states can hold only for a limited period of time. Anticipation cannot extend so far into the future that it undermines memory of the past. By the same token, there cannot be so much stored memory of past events that it comes at the expense of our ability to anticipate and plan for the future. A break in this equilibrium would . . . undermine our ability to sustain long-term projects by breaking the unity of forward- and backward-looking attitudes necessary to ground these projects.

In effect, the problem with increasing the lifespan is not that it causes psychology and biology to part company. Rather, changing the biology of human aging would profoundly change human psychology.

Psychological Effects

On one level, then, Glannon's concern about using stem cell therapies to significantly increase the human lifespan is a consequentialist worry about the psychological effects on humans of dissociating the present from the distant past or remote future. According to Glannon, we cannot rationally desire to lengthen the human life span because doing so would have disastrous consequences for our ability to undertake projects, accept responsibility for our past or future actions, or indeed, even care very much about "our" future. Notice, however, that there is a corollary to Glannon's maxim, as reformulated. If a new biology gives rise to a new psychology, it also gives rise to a new ethics. Or to put the point negatively, a new biology threatens our existing ethical commitments.

It is this kind of thought that animates the opposition of the life cycle traditionalists to biotechnologies that might alter the trajectory of a human life. When Leon Kass says that "many human goods . . . are inseparable from our aging bodies, from our living in time, and from the natural life cycle," he has this worry in mind. It is also a central concern of *Our Posthuman Future*. Fukuyama suggests that we can grasp the threat biotechnology poses by noting the pervasiveness in modern moral discourse of the language of human rights, which is effectively the only available vocabulary for discussing human goods or ends. The most persuasive account of human rights, however, is framed in relation to the notion of a stable human nature. According to Fukuyama, neither a religious conception of rights nor a positivist conception is viable. But once we recognize the relationship between human rights and human nature, we can give a very precise sense to the worry that we may be heading toward a posthuman future. The fear is that biotechnology will change the species-typical characteristics shared by all humans. If that happens, and if rights are tied to a conception of human nature that is in turn rooted in a biological reality, then biotechnology threatens the very basis of human morality as we know it.

> *"Certainly we should scrutinize stem cell research . . . but to argue it should not proceed on the basis that human rights depend on an immutable biology is to engage in a logic of infinite regress."*

Stem Cell Treatments Do Not Threaten Human Morality

Susan Squier, Catherine Waldby, and Anita Silvers

The following two-part viewpoint by Susan Squier, Catherine Waldby, and Anita Silvers challenges the preceding viewpoint's perspective that stem cell treatments threaten the concept of what it means to be human. In Part I, Squier and Waldby argue that there is no "natural" life span. They point out that people living in the developing world have been relying on biomedical advances to extend life span for years. In Part II, Silvers challenges the notion that morality is grounded in sameness and cross species stem cell research challenges this sameness. She argues that a morality grounded in sameness is actually immoral. Squier is a professor of English and women's studies at Pennsylvania State University. Waldby teaches medical sociology at the

Susan Squier, Catherine Waldby, and Anita Silvers, "Letters to the Editor," *The Hastings Center Report*, vol. 35, November–December 2005, pp. 4–8. Copyright © 2005 Hastings Center. Reproduced by permission.

University of New South Wales in Australia, and Anita Silvers is a professor of philosophy at San Francisco State University.

As you read, consider the following questions:

1. Why might people living in developed countries have a different life trajectory than people who live in developing countries, according to Squier and Waldby?
2. What, according to these authors, is an example of a biomedical achievement that is humanizing?
3. What does Silvers think happens when biological typicality becomes an overarching value?

Part I

Paul Lauritzen . . . is certainly right in urging us to move toward an "expansive view of technology" in order to escape the "narrowly focused . . . repetitive and rigid" quality of much existing debate over stem cell research. Yet Lauritzen's otherwise insightful essay still betrays some narrowness, both in its assertion that the broader perspective on such biomedical technologies is merely "beginning to emerge," and in its assumption that our ethical commitments—grounded as they are in the notion of "natural human life"—are not subject to productive critique and reformulation.

Debate Has Been Proceeding

Had he followed his own advice and moved beyond what he calls the typical frame of bioethics to consider the "cultural space that art provides for moral reflection on social issues posed by definitions of nature," he would have discovered that the history of popular debate over the social and moral impact of biogenetic research and therapy is a long and rich one. As Squier has explored in *Babies in Bottles* (1994) and *Liminal Lives* (2004), the question of the implications of a wide variety of biomedical interventions into the human lifespan has en-

Creating Chimeras

Created by injecting the embryonic stem cells of one or more species into the embryo of another species and then allowing that embryo to continue development in the womb of either species, a biological chimera is a way to hybridize two or more species that won't cross sexually. The exact results are largely unpredictable except for the certainty that the chimera will contain cells of each species proportionate to the numbers placed in the embryo. A creature made from an equal number of cells from two species could look like one species but contain the genes, organs, and intelligence of the other.

Mark Dowie, "Gods and Monsters,"
January/February 2004. www.motherjones.com.

gaged novelists, playwrights, journalists, and embryologist-poets, as well as zoologists, geneticists, crystallographers, philosophers, and physicians, since the early twentieth century.

Why does Lauritzen believe the debate has just begun? Perhaps because he writes in an era when the popular forum referred to has been replaced by conversations among experts whose disciplinary positions (as scientists, doctors, theologians, and bioethicists) give them the authority to be heard. Relying on experts to gauge the impact of new biomedical technologies keeps us from considering their full consequences. Instead, since we have declared the testimony of those who are not experts off-limits, we are limited to gauging the level of acceptable risk posed.

Lauritzen's article argues that biotechnological innovation represents a threat to human rights—biotechnology will change the species-typical characteristics shared by all humans, and thus the biological basis for human nature. The problem with stem cell research to Lauritzen is it may significantly extend the life span and change the natural trajectory of human life "that moves through youth and adulthood toward old age and finally, decline and death." This, he fears, would alter the kinds of social relations and mutual obligations associated with aging, illness, reproduction, and death.

There Is No Natural Human Trajectory

We regard the grounding of human rights in a natural trajectory of human biology as highly problematic. The trajectory he posits is not natural, if by *natural* we mean uncontaminated by technology. The life trajectory in which a person lives for seventy or so years, is healthy in childhood and adulthood, and declines only in old age is utterly dependant on a vast biomedical research and clinical infrastructure: dental care, antibiotic medication, diagnostic and screening technology, vaccination, regulatory standards—the list is endless. These technological interventions protect those who live in the developed world from the infectious epidemics, parasitic invasions, malnutrition, and sheer risk that threatens the viability of life at any point among the poor in the developing world. The life trajectory Lauritzen assumes is natural and species-typical is in fact a product of social wealth, biotechnical intervention, and the sheer flexibility and mutability of biology, its responsiveness to change, and instrumentalization.

Biotechnology: Noble and Ignoble Achievements

Furthermore, while Lauritzen associates biotechnical intervention with dehumanization and loss of moral foundations, we argue that medicine's tendency to treat the body as matter to be manipulated does not have straightforward ethical implications. This tendency is the basis of all great humanist achievements of biomedicine, as well as all its ignominious moments. It forms the basis, for example, for both organ donation and eugenic sterilization of the disabled in the 1930s. Certainly we should scrutinize stem cell research for the ethics and politics of its possible applications, but to argue it should not proceed on the basis that human rights depend on an immutable biology is to engage in a logic of infinite regress.

Although we indicate the limitations of Lauritzen's argument, we also affirm the important contribution it makes. By drawing attention to the broader cultural conversation about social and ethical consequences of biotechnology, Lauritzen expands the frame available to his discipline, disregarding the narrow rules that limit significant contributions to those deemed "expert." The result could be a more genuinely representative public debate on the meaning of these new biotechnologies—for us as human beings, for other living beings, and for the Earth whose precious space we share.

Part II

In "Stem Cells, Biotechnology, and Human Rights: Implications for a Posthuman Future," Paul Lauritzen ratchets up the threat that regenerative biology is supposed to pose. Being able to regenerate deteriorating or destroyed tissue will weaken human rights, he contends. The following speculations are extrapolated from his discussion:

Why Is "Natural" Right?

First, to alter the species typicality of the human body is to treat humans as mere malleable material. Such practice fails to appreciate the "natural contours" of human biology as being intrinsically valuable ends. Lauritzen does not explain why what is "natural" must be right. But this equation might undergird claims to medical interventions that maintain or return patients to species-typical condition. If so, challenging the value he places on species typicality could attenuate commitments to preventative and therapeutic health care.

Second, to acknowledge human vulnerability is to see our own needy selves in other people's neediness; thus is compassion for the needy nourished. But with viable methods of biological regeneration, people's physical vulnerability will recede. By diminishing human neediness, regenerative medicine might short-circuit people's commitments to protect each other.

Finally, to confront people with the innovative entities that bioengineering could make is to blunt their intuition of how humans are supposed to be. This intuition promotes moral connectedness. People are especially connected to what is biologically closest to themselves, their family, or their tribe. But biological homogeneity also links people who are less closely related by underwriting reciprocal moral claims that apply within, but not beyond, the human species. The disposition to connect with strangers might collapse if stressed by encounters with entities that straddle species' boundaries.

Biological Sameness

Lauritzen takes biological sameness to ground commitment, compassion, and connectedness, and therefore human rights. This is bad news for biologically anomalous people—individuals whose biological condition deviates markedly from species typicality. For how will such people fare on a theory that situates moral value in our all being the same? Lauritzen observes that claims about what is essential to being human often are used to exclude groups from full membership in the moral community. Unfortunately, he does not explain how to block such results.

If species typicality is the prevailing value, human rights become mere routes to resources for achieving typicality. Further, as history shows, when species typicality becomes a social and political end, stigmatization follows for people whom medicine cannot make biologically typical. The conceptual divisions Lauritzen endorses thus lead to unfairness and discrimination, not equal rights.

Take the matter of segregating athletes who use prosthetics. Bicycle racer Dory Selinger lost a foot and wears a prosthetic that does not sacrifice pedaling power to ankle flexion. With it, Selinger has raced just ten seconds off the world record but may compete only in the Paralympics because his foot is not "natural."

Not all similar enhancements are artificial. [Cyclist] Lance Armstrong also enjoys advantageous lower extremities—atypically long thigh bones that give him more pedal power. Unlike Selinger's, his advantage is acclaimed because it is "natural." Were his thigh bones prosthetic, he too would be stigmatized by being segregated.

Embrace the Atypical

Allowing allegiance to "nature" to eclipse fairness, talent, courage, and persistence holds no promise for securing human rights. Compassion, commitment, and connectedness require reaching out to others despite their differences. These dispositions won't survive being filtered through a conceptual screen that demands sameness.

We should embrace, not be repelled by, photographs of human ears growing on the backs of mice because these are being made as transplants for people born without ears. What's really repugnant about growing ears on mice is the social necessity for doing so—namely, to save these people from being stigmatized for being atypical.

And how ironic that research into therapies meant mainly to restore individuals to species typicality faces such fearful speculation. For centuries, medical research has enabled human bodies to surpass their functional capabilities, but functional enhancement has never reduced the role of rights. To the contrary, the idea that nations should subscribe to global human rights has grown in influence as the authority of biological standardization waned.

Approaching human rights from a perspective that idolizes sameness thus seems counterproductive for morality. Lauritzen is exactly right to worry about how inhumanity is surfacing in the debate about regenerative medicine. But his advice is exactly wrong, for the antidote to inhumanity surely is not to draw exclusionary boundaries and deny hope.

> *"Moralists concerned about human em-
> bryos should welcome and support [Al-
> tered Nuclear Transfer–Oocyte Assisted
> Reprogramming]."*

Altered Nuclear Transfer
Is a Moral Way to Obtain
Embryonic Stem Cells

E. Christian Brugger

*In the following viewpoint, E. Christian Brugger discusses the
proposal called Altered Nuclear Transfer–Oocyte Assisted Reprogramming (ANT-OAR), which attempts to circumvent the moral
objections to embryonic stem cell research. The ANT-OAR procedure alters a human egg cell (an oocyte) so that the egg cell is
not able to produce all the genes necessary for the complete development of a human being. Such an egg cell, however, can be
used to produce an "embryo-like" entity, from which embryonic
stem cells can be extracted. Brugger argues that the ANT-OAR
procedure will allow scientists to produce "moral" stem cells, and
he goes on to refute the basis for opposition to the procedure.
Brugger is a philosopher and theologian at the Institute for the
Psychological Sciences in Arlington, Virginia.*

E. Christian Brugger, "Moral Stem Cells," *First Things*, May 2006. Copyright © 2006
Institute on Religion and Public Life. All rights reserved. Reproduced by permission.

As you read, consider the following questions:

1. What is Brugger's description of how the identity and function of each cell in the human body is determined?

2. What do the opponents of ANT-OAR fear will be created, in the author's opinion?

3. What does Brugger say is the difference between totipotent and pluripotent cells?

The desire of the scientific community for embryonic stem cells is not diminishing. Indeed, it is increasing, despite promising research with adult stem cells (scientists have already developed therapies for more than fifty diseases and disorders using stem cells from bone marrow and umbilical cord blood) and despite the fact that no useful embryonic stem-cell-based therapies currently exist or are even in FDA [Food and Drug Administration] clinical trials.

Indeed, no amount of success in clinical trials using adult stem cells is likely to lessen the desire of the scientific community for embryonic stem cells—which is what has created the arguments that have dominated the medical news since 2001. For a large swath of the nation, creating human embryos (with the intent to experiment lethally upon them) is morally repugnant, but the scientific community seems unwilling to accept anything else.

Obtaining Stem Cells Without Killing Embryos

But what if we could produce pluripotent stem cells, functionally identical to embryonic stem cells, without ever needing to create, experiment on, and destroy human embryos?

This is what a scientific procedure called "Altered Nuclear Transfer–Oocyte Assisted Reprogramming" (ANT-OAR) proposes to do. The proposal is based upon the premise that the identity and function of each cell in the human body depends, in the first place, on which subset of the approximately thirty thousand genes in the cell's nucleus is switched on or off. In other words, the gene sequence is *not* what is responsible for determining cellular identity, since the DNA is identical in nearly every cell in the human body. Rather it is the *programming* of the gene sequence that distinguishes cell types. This genetic programming is referred to as the cell's "epigenetic state."

We know the key epigenetic markers of pluripotent stem cells, and we know the markers of zygotes, which are one-celled human embryos. The stem cells that scientists seek are "pluripotent" (with the capacity of a cell to develop into most all the tissue types of the human body), while zygotes are "totipotent" (with the capacity to develop *all* the tissues of the human body, and extra-embryonic supporting tissues like the placenta, in an organized and self-directed manner). Using a procedure called "somatic cell nuclear transfer," defenders of ANT-OAR propose extracting the nucleus of a somatic cell (an adult body cell with the highly specified "epigenetic state" of the cell type from which it was extracted, say a skin cell) and then transferring it into an ooplast (an organic sac of cytoplasm left when the nucleus has been removed from an egg cell, or oocyte).

Human Embryos Not Created in ANT-OAR

In the ANT-OAR proposal, *before* we transferred the somatic cell nucleus into the ooplast, we would preemptively alter its epigenetic state so that the genes expressed in the nuclear genome are consistent with pluripotent stem cells—but incompatible with totipotency and thus with the existence of a human zygote.

When scientists attempt cloning, they similarly remove the nucleus from an egg cell and insert a new nucleus. And they have discovered that the biochemical constituents in oocyte cytoplasm have the remarkable capacity to reprogram the epigenetic state of a transferred nucleus back to a state of totipo-

Stem Cell Advances May Make Moral Issue Moot

If only human embryonic stem cells could sprout anew from something other than a human embryo. Researchers could harvest them and perhaps harness their great biomedical potential without destroying what some consider to be a budding human life.

But like a low-calorie banana split or the proverbial free lunch, there is no such thing as an embryo-free embryonic stem cell.

Or is there?...

The gathering consensus among biologists is that embryonic stem cells are made, not born—and that embryos are not an essential ingredient. That means that today's heated debates over embryo rights could fade in the aftermath of technical advances allowing scientists to convert ordinary cells into embryonic stem cells.

Rick Weiss, June 6, 2005. www.washingtonpost.com.

tency. When the nucleus is transferred, the cytoplasm goes to work on the genome, and we are back to a totipotent zygote—the one-celled embryo whose moral status has caused so much concern.

For ANT-OAR, the key element in avoiding this is the *altered* nuclear transfer: The genetic material in the nucleus is preemptively altered to prevent its being affected by the reprogramming of the oocyte cytoplasm. The result is that the nuclear genome will never reach a state of totipotency—and thus we would create a pluripotent stem cell (from which, if all goes well, stem-cell lines can be derived) without ever creating a human embryo....

Critics

But there remain critics of the proposal. David Schindler, dean of the John Paul II Institute in Washington, D.C., has emerged as the principal Catholic critic of ANT-OAR. In the pages of *Communio*, several essays have appeared . . . with defenders of altered nuclear transfer on one side, and with Schindler and his followers on the other.

These opponents of ANT-OAR fear the procedure will create, not a pluripotent stem cell, but merely a badly disabled human embryo. Faced with the question of how can it be an embryo when it has the biological characteristics of a pluripotent stem cell, Schindler replies that he does not dispute that the *end result* of the process is a pluripotent stem cell; what he fears is that the entity brought into existence at the *beginning* of the process is a human embryo.

Concerns About Conception

As it happens, the ANT-OAR proposal emerges from the same moral concerns that worry critics such as Schindler: It cannot be right to create human entities like embryos solely for the purpose of destroying them and extracting their components. So, the defenders hold, the entity brought into existence must look and act like a pluripotent stem cell in every relevant respect in order to be considered morally acceptable; if through animal trials the product exhibits embryonic characteristics, the procedure will be rejected.

The problem, for the critics, is in the way pluripotent stem cells would be created in ANT-OAR. Because the procedure is a form of somatic cell nuclear transfer, its product, Schindler argues, comes into existence in a "species-specific way." The process of ANT-OAR entails the fusing of an ooplast with a diploid somatic cell nucleus. In Schindler's view, this fusion is tantamount, in its effect, to conception.

In fact, he calls it a "mimicked conception." The fertilization of an egg by a sperm brings into existence a single-celled entity whose progenitor cells include an oocyte, and that possesses a complete human genome contained in a diploid nucleus. So, too, somatic cell nuclear transfer used to clone human embryos brings into existence a single-celled entity whose progenitor cells include an oocyte and that possesses a complete human genome contained in a diploid nucleus. And ANT-OAR *also* brings into existence a single-celled entity whose progenitor cells include an oocyte and whose diploid nucleus contains a complete human genome. Whenever we fuse an enucleated oocyte and a diploid nucleus, we "mimic conception"—bringing into existence an entity in a species-specific way and thus creating something that must be a human embryo.

ANT-OAR Entity Is Not Human

This seems to mean that, for Schindler, the epigenetic state—the programming of the nuclear genome—is irrelevant to the nature of the entity. How this could be so is hard to see. The entity brought into existence through ANT-OAR is *not* totipotent until the specialized epigenetic state of the somatic cell nucleus is reprogrammed through its interaction with the oocyte cytoplasm, and, through preemptive genetic alterations, ANT-OAR sets out to prevent a state of totipotency from ever being realized.

Is it reasonable to hold, as Schindler does, that the entity brought into existence is *in any case* a human embryo? He claims that it is the embryo itself that directs its own epigenetic reprogramming back to a state of totipotency. ANT-OAR, he believes, can modify only the end of the process (to a state of totipotency or pluripotency, etc.), and thus the nature of the entity that originally came into existence in a species-specific way remains a human embryo.

The answer to Schindler's kind of complaint seems obvious. An entity is a human embryo only if the organic material is *able to be human*—if, in the language of Aristotle, it is *apt* to receive a substantial human form. Not every collection of organic material, even material that includes an oocyte and a diploid nucleus, can be a human being. We know this because we know that teratomas (naturally occurring tumors)—together with hydatidiform moles (disorganized entities that occur in humans and other animals as a result of certain types of defects in fertilization) and even oocytes themselves—are not human embryos, yet they all have as their starting material an oocyte and a diploid nucleus.

With respect to the biological conditions for the origins of a human zygote, this means the single-celled entity brought into existence must possess the inherent active biological disposition for self-directed development toward species maturity (including the capacity to develop all tissue types necessary for a differentiated human body and extra-embryonic supporting materials). In other words, the cell must be characterized by an epigenetic state of totipotency.

Biologically speaking, totipotency in a cell is a necessary and sufficient condition for concluding that that cell is a human embryo. It follows that even in human cloning, a human embryo does not come into existence until—among other things—the nuclear genome, through the reprogramming that takes place as a result of its interaction with oocyte cytoplasm, has attained a state of totipotency. The entity *immediately* after nuclear transfer and before nuclear reprogramming is *not* a human embryo that begins to self-direct its own process of reprogramming. Rather, it is akin to a body cell, with the epigenetic makeup of the donor somatic cell.

This suggests that the efficient cause of the reprogramming is *not* an embryo; the efficient cause is the complex of active constituents in the oocyte cytoplasm—the cytoplasm reprograms the nucleus. The product remains a single isolated cell until a state of totipotency is attained, at which point a human organism—a new whole, embryonic human being—comes into existence. In the case of ANT-OAR, the product never is totipotent. It is never apt to receive a substantial human form, and therefore it never becomes a human embryo.

Doubt Not Justified

One might still ask: Given the novelty of the procedure, its likeness in certain respects to human cloning, and the complexity and mystery of the progenitor cells used for its starting materials, isn't some doubt about the identity of the product of ANT-OAR justified? And if it is, are we not required to side with caution and refuse to proceed with experimentation that might produce disabled embryos?

If doubt were justified, then such caution would, in fact, be required. But ANT-OAR, as its defenders propose it, warrants no such doubt. It aims to create a cell that, from its first moment, exhibits organic properties biologically *incompatible* with totipotency. Schindler asserts that a single-celled entity can at once be a human embryo and yet manifestly not be (or ever have been) characterized by an epigenetic state of totipotency.

That requires one to believe that a cell's epigenetic identity is not a necessary condition for cellular identity—which, in turn, requires a dualistic anthropology inconsistent with the Christian understanding of humanity. It denies that the biological disposition of the organic material is a necessary condition for determining cellular identity. It implicitly holds that a cell can biologically look and behave in ways biologically indicative of a certain cell type, yet in fact be a wholly different kind of cell.

The property distinguishing a liver cell from a cardiac cell, or a retinal cell from a skin cell, is the programming of the genome. Yet no one would argue that a cardiac cell is a liver cell, or that a retinal cell is a skin cell, or that any of them are human embryos. The assumption that epigenetic identity does not determine cellular identity is clearly false—and moralists concerned about human embryos should welcome and support ANT-OAR as it moves to testing with animal cells.

Periodical Bibliography

The following articles have been selected to supplement the diverse views presented in this chapter.

Susan Kerr Bernal   "A Massive Snowball of Fraud and Deceit," *Journal of Andrology*, May/June 2006.

Alan Boyle   "Stem-Cell Pioneer Does a Reality Check," *MSNBC.com.*, June 22, 2005. www.msnbc.msn.com.

Malcom Byrnes and Jose Granados   "ANT-OAR Fails on All Counts," *Science & Theology News*, July 13, 2006.

Joe Carter   "Hype and Hypocrisy: Kinsley, IVF, and Embryo Destruction," *Evangelical Outpost*, July 10, 2006.

Michael Cook   "To Clone or Not to Clone," *Mercatornet.com*, December 6, 2005. www.mercatornet.com.

Rebecca Dresser   "Stem Cell Research, the Bigger Picture," *Perspectives in Biology and Medicine*, Spring 2005.

Steven J. DuBord   "Heading for the Island," *New American*, August 22, 2005.

Nicholas Jackson   "Embryonic Stem Cell Research: Shades of the Third Reich," *Sierra Times*, June 27, 2005.

Michael Kinsley   "False Dilemma on Stem Cells," *Washington Post*, July 7, 2006.

Liza Mundy   "Souls on Ice: America's Embryo Glut and the Wasted Promise of Stem Cell Research," *MotherJones*, July/August 2006.

Jason Scott Robert   "The Science and Ethics of Making Part Human Animals in Stem Cell Biology," *The FASEB Journal*, 2006.

OPPOSING
VIEWPOINTS®
SERIES

CHAPTER 3

What Role Should the Government Play in Stem Cell Research?

Chapter Preface

The U.S. government typically functions as a financer and overseer of scientific research. It funds the majority of basic research, or research that provides the fundamental knowledge that practical research builds upon, in the United States. In this capacity, the federal government can speed up or stifle research by controlling the level of funding an area of research receives. Additionally, researchers who accept federal money are obligated to comply with the rules and regulations of several federal agencies, such as the Food and Drug Administration (FDA) and the National Institutes of Health (NIH). In this way, federal regulators monitor research to ensure it is conducted ethically. The U.S. Congress and each U.S. president since Ronald Reagan (1981–1989) have wrestled with the question of whether to provide federal funding for research using cells from developing humans: embryonic or fetal, including stem cells.

The U.S. government began regulating fetal research in the 1970s and generally makes a distinction between fetal research and fetal tissue research. Federal lawmakers motivated by the abuses of the Tuskegee Syphilis Study, where hundreds of African American males were denied treatment for syphilis, enacted the National Research Act of 1974. The act put in place several important provisions to protect "human subjects" used in biomedical research and included provisions specifically prohibiting federally funded research on aborted fetuses. These provisions were included to prevent the "dehumanization of unborn children" and were in response to the landmark *Roe v. Wade* Supreme Court decision that legalized abortion in 1973. Also in 1973, the Uniform Anatomical Gift Act was enacted, which regulates the use of human organs and tissues after death. Under this act, fetal tissue cannot be sold for profit and cannot be used for any reason except research or therapeutic purposes.

During the 1970s and for most of the 1980s fetal tissue research progressed, using tissue from aborted fetuses. In the late 80s, however, scientists began experimenting with tissue transplants and were transplanting fetal cells and tissues into the brains of victims of Parkinson's disease. Prompted by this new development—where fetal tissue is used not just as a research tool but as transplantation material—the administration of President Reagan declared a moratorium on all federal funding for fetal tissue research.

The moratorium lasted for five years. Within the first weeks of taking office in 1993, President Bill Clinton reversed a number of policies that had been established under the preceding Republican administrations of Reagan and George H.W. Bush. One of the first directives Clinton issued was to end the federal moratorium on the use of fetal tissue for federally funded medical research. Later that year the U.S. Congress followed suit and enacted a law (the NIH Revitalization Act) to allow federally funded fetal tissue research. Today, federal funding for fetal tissue transplantation research is allowed under strict guidelines.

The U.S. government began regulating embryonic research in the 1990s. For a brief period of time, research using human embryos was allowed; authorized under the NIH Revitalization Act of 1993. A few short years later, however, the U.S. Congress prohibited funding for any research that harms an embryo—a prohibition that essentially blocks all federal funding for the initial step of stem cell research, where stem cells are extracted from embryos. That is where things stood until August 9, 2001, when President George W. Bush made his famous announcement saying, "I have concluded that we should allow federal funds to be used for research on existing stem cell lines, where the life and death decision has already been made." Thus, as of 2006 only research on stem cell lines that were in existence on August 9, 2001, may receive federal funding.

In 2005 and 2006, the U.S. Congress attempted to expand the number of stem cell lines eligible for federal funding. The U.S. Stem Cell Research Enhancement Act of 2005 would have allowed federally funded researchers to extract stem cells frozen in in vitro fertilized (IVF) embryos and create new stem cell lines from them. The legislation passed both the House and the Senate; however, when it was placed on President Bush's desk, he vetoed it. Today (in 2007), the federal policy on funding embryonic stem cell research remains as it was in 2001.

The government's role in research using the tissues of developing humans is a subject that will probably be debated by presidents and Congress for years to come. The authors of the viewpoints in the following chapter discuss what role they believe the government should have in stem cell research.

*"In 2001, [President Bush] set forth a
new policy on stem cell research that
struck a balance between the needs of
science and the demands of conscience."*

U.S. Stem Cell Policy Is Moral

George W. Bush

*In the following viewpoint, President George W. Bush explains to
the American public why he vetoed a bill, the U.S. Stem Cell Research Enhancement Act of 2005, which would have changed the
U.S. policy on stem cell research by allowing the use of federal
funds to create new stem cell lines. The president claims that his
policy is balanced between morality and the needs of science. He
contends that it is moral because it does not support the further
destruction of embryos, but it tries to derive some good by funding research on embryos that had already been destroyed, and
thus it meets the needs of science. Bush was the first U.S. president to allow the funding of any embryonic stem cell research.
He announced his policy on August 9, 2001.*

As you read, consider the following questions:

1. What does Bush say is the reason he signed the Fetus
   Farming and Prohibition Act?

George W. Bush, remarks on stem cell research policy, July 19, 2006. www.whitehouse
.gov.

2. According to the president, how many human embryonic stem cell lines were in use in 2006 and eligible for federal funding?

3. What is one technique to produce versatile stem cells that scientists are exploring and that does not involve embryo destruction, according to Bush?

Congress has . . . passed and sent to my desk two bills concerning the use of stem cells in biomedical research. These bills illustrate both the promise and perils we face in the age of biotechnology. In this new era, our challenge is to harness the power of science to ease human suffering without sanctioning the practices that violate the dignity of human life.

Funding for Research

In 2001, I spoke to the American people and set forth a new policy on stem cell research that struck a balance between the needs of science and the demands of conscience. When I took office, there was no federal funding for human embryonic stem cell research. Under the policy I announced [in 2001], my administration became the first to make federal funds available for this research, yet only on embryonic stem cell lines derived from embryos that had already been destroyed.

My administration has made available more than $90 million for research on these lines. This policy has allowed important research to go forward without using taxpayer funds to encourage the further deliberate destruction of human embryos.

One of the bills Congress has passed [the Fetus Farming Prohibition Act] builds on the progress we have made [since 2001]. So I signed it into law. Congress has also passed a second bill that attempts to overturn the balanced policy I set. This bill [the Stem Cell Research Enhancement Act of 2005] would support the taking of innocent human life in the hope of finding medical benefits for others. It crosses a moral boundary that our decent society needs to respect, so I vetoed it.

Like all Americans, I believe our nation must vigorously pursue the tremendous possibility that science offers to cure disease and improve the lives of millions. We have opportunities to discover cures and treatments that were unthinkable generations ago. Some scientists believe that one source of these cures might be embryonic stem cell research. Embryonic stem cells have the ability to grow into specialized adult tissues, and this may give them the potential to replace damaged or defective cells or body parts and treat a variety of diseases.

We All Began as Embryos

Yet we must also remember that embryonic stem cells come from human embryos that are destroyed for their cells. Each of these human embryos is a unique human life with inherent dignity and matchless value. We see that value in the children who are with us today. Each of these children began his or her life as a frozen embryo that was created for in vitro fertilization, but remained unused after the fertility treatments were complete. Each of these children was adopted while still an embryo, and has been blessed with the chance to grow up in a loving family.

These boys and girls are not spare parts. They remind us of what is lost when embryos are destroyed in the name of research. They remind us that we all begin our lives as a small collection of cells. And they remind us that in our zeal for new treatments and cures, America must never abandon our fundamental morals.

Some people argue that finding new cures for disease requires the destruction of human embryos like the ones that these families adopted. I disagree. I believe that with the right techniques and the right policies, we can achieve scientific progress while living up to our ethical responsibilities. That's what I sought in 2001, when I set forth my administration's policy allowing federal funding for research on embryonic stem cell lines where the life-and-death decision had already been made.

No Ban on Embryonic Stem Cell Research

This balanced approach has worked. Under this policy, 21 human embryonic stem cell lines are currently in use in research that is eligible for federal funding. Each of these lines can be replicated many times. And as a result, the National Institutes of Health have helped make more than 700 shipments to researchers since 2001. There is no ban on embryonic stem cell research. To the contrary, even critics of my policy concede that these federally funded lines are being used in research every day by scientists around the world. My policy has allowed us to explore the potential of embryonic stem cells, and it has allowed America to continue to lead the world in this area.

Advances in Research

Since I announced my policy in 2001, advances in scientific research have also shown the great potential of stem cells that are derived without harming human embryos. My administration has expanded the funding of research into stem cells that can be drawn from children, adults, and the blood in umbilical cords, with no harm to the donor. And these stem cells are already being used in medical treatments.

With us today are patients who have benefited from treatments with adult and umbilical-cord-blood stem cells. . . .

They are living proof that effective medical science can also be ethical. Researchers are now also investigating new techniques that could allow doctors and scientists to produce stem cells just as versatile as those derived from human embryos. One technique scientists are exploring would involve reprogramming an adult cell; for example, [programming] a skin cell to function like an embryonic stem cell. Science of-

Leftover Lives

Zara was one of those "leftover" human embryos that we read about so often in today's news—the ones that some scientists and celebrities want to destroy to obtain embryonic stem cells for their so-far fruitless embryonic stem cell research.

That means that Zara could have been a science experiment. But she's not. She's a blue-eyed blonde with a million-dollar smile. Her life was rescued through embryo adoption—a relatively new concept with which mainstream America is largely unaware.

Dorinda Bordlee, National Review Online,
May 23, 2005.

fers the hope that we may one day enjoy the potential benefits of embryonic stem cells without destroying human life.

We must continue to explore these hopeful alternatives and advance the cause of scientific research while staying true to the ideals of a decent and humane society. The bill . . . upholds these humane ideals and draws an important ethical line to guide our research. The Fetus Farming Prohibition Act was sponsored by Senators [Rick] Santorum and [Sam] Brownback . . . and by Congressman Dave Weldon, along with [Congressman] Nathan Deal. . . . This good law prohibits one of the most egregious abuses in biomedical research, the trafficking in human fetuses that are created with the sole intent of aborting them to harvest their parts. Human beings are not a raw material to be exploited, or a commodity to be bought or sold, and this bill will help ensure that we respect the fundamental ethical line. . . .

No Funding for Deliberate Destruction of Embryos

Unfortunately, Congress has sent me a bill that fails to meet this ethical test. This legislation would overturn the balanced policy on embryonic stem cell research that my administration has followed [since 2001]. This bill would also undermine the principle that Congress, itself, has followed for more than a decade, when it has prohibited federal funding for research that destroys human embryos.

If this bill would have become law, American taxpayers would, for the first time in our history, be compelled to fund the deliberate destruction of human embryos. And I'm not going to allow it. . . .

I made it clear to the Congress that I will not allow our nation to cross this moral line. I felt like crossing this line would be a mistake, and once crossed, we would find it almost impossible to turn back. Crossing the line would needlessly encourage a conflict between science and ethics that can only do damage to both, and to our nation as a whole. If we're to find the right ways to advance ethical medical research, we must also be willing, when necessary, to reject the wrong ways. . . .

Science Should Serve Humanity

As science brings us ever closer to unlocking the secrets of human biology, it also offers temptations to manipulate human life and violate human dignity. Our conscience and history as a nation demand that we resist this temptation. America was founded on the principle that we are all created equal, and endowed by our Creator with the right to life. We can advance the cause of science while upholding this founding promise. We can harness the promise of technology without becoming slaves to technology. And we can ensure that science serves the cause of humanity instead of the other way around.

America pursues medical advances in the name of life, and we will achieve the great breakthroughs we all seek with reverence for the gift of life. I believe America's scientists have the ingenuity and skill to meet this challenge.

"Not only was Bush's science wrong [regarding embryonic stem cell research], the ethics behind his so-called compromise were deeply flawed, too."

U.S. Stem Cell Policy Is Morally Inconsistent

Arthur Caplan

In the following viewpoint, Arthur Caplan contends that U.S. policy toward stem cell research as outlined by President George W. Bush in August 2001 is deeply flawed. Caplan claims that the moral basis of the policy—specifically, that it is moral to use stem cells taken from embryos that have already been destroyed, but it is immoral to allow the further destruction of embryos—is inconsistent. Caplan maintains that the Bush policy conflicts with what most scientists, disease advocacy organizations, the majority of Americans, and a number of other countries believe: The government should support embryonic stem cell research. Arthur Caplan is a professor of bioethics and the director of the Center for Bioethics at the University of Pennsylvania.

As you read, consider the following questions:

1. What does the author say that President Bush and Karl Rove know best about?

Arthur Caplan, "Bush to Stem Cell Community: Drop Dead," MSNBC, July 19, 2006. www.msnbc.msn.com. Reproduced by permission.

2. According to Caplan, how many stem cell lines did President Bush say held "great promise"?

3. According to the author, who benefits most from stem cell research?

President Bush's embryonic stem cell policy began with lies and has now ended with one.

Bush reserved his first veto as president for one of the only valuable things this do-almost-nothing Congress has managed to actually get done.

With a flourish of a veto pen that has remained dormant no matter how dopey Congress has been, the Senate bill allowing public funding of embryonic stem cell research has been consigned to the legislative trash can.

2001 Policy

An administration that has shown itself over and over again to have trouble telling the truth is now telling Americans in wheelchairs, those with damaged hearts, babies who are diabetic and those left immobile by Parkinsonism not to worry. The president, whose grasp of science left him unable to identify creationism as a fundamentally religious idea, and his trusty sidekick [presidential adviser] Karl Rove, rarely seen in a white lab coat but who knows something about rats, having been in Washington for some time now, claim to know best which medical research is most likely to benefit diseased Americans in the future.

When Bush uttered his first confused words on the subject of embryonic stem cell research . . . in August 2001, he said that he was opposed to embryonic stem cell research since it involved the destruction of human life.

He noted that there were embryos, and many of them, already in existence in infertility clinics and left unwanted by those who created them. But he held it was wrong to use those in research. Instead, he told us, he had found a way out of the dilemma of how to do embryonic stem cell research without destroying any embryos.

What had Bush figured out that no one in the scientific community could see then and remains unable to see now?

There were, he said, 60 stem cell lines that had been made from embryos which held "great promise that could lead to breakthrough therapies and cures." If he gave federal money to support research on those lines and funded research on adult stem cells, such as bone marrow, fetal blood cells taken from umbilical cords and other adult stem cells found in skin, muscle and the intestine, then all would be well.

Wrong Science, Flawed Ethics

The president's supporters, a much larger set then than now, blessed his insight and his wisdom in producing a marvelous "compromise" and pronounced the quandary over stem cell research resolved.

Except, as even the president must have known and some of his most vocal supporters knew, the president was talking through his hat.

There were never 60 embryonic stem cell lines available for research. Not even close. Even if there had been, that number would never have been enough to support serious research on diseases and disorders for very long, as experts in embryonic stem cell research found out in less than a year.

Not only was Bush's science wrong, the ethics behind his so-called compromise were deeply flawed, too.

If the president deemed it moral to use cell lines made from human embryos that had already been destroyed, then why would he argue that other embryos headed inevitably for destruction couldn't be the source of new stem cell lines?

In fact, if the president was so concerned about the fate of embryos, why did he not speak out to close infertility programs around the country that destroy embryos? Why did he not try to shut down privately funded embryonic stem cell re-

© 2001 DAYTON DAILY NEWS—
grimmy.com

NO STEM CELLS WERE HURT IN THE MAKING OF THIS DECISION.

search? And, if the president was so worried about destructive embryo research, why did he not propose a ban on bringing across our borders any cure or therapy that might be discovered overseas if it was based on embryonic stem cell research?

If adult stem cell research were really an alternative to embryonic [stem cell research], then why have nearly all but the tiniest handful of the experts who work on stem cells maintained that this is false? And why has the president failed to secure the agreement of a single medical or scientific society of any standing with his position that a combination of funding a small number of existing stem cell lines made from human embryos and a push behind adult stem cell research is the best strategy to mend damaged brains and heal broken spinal cords?

Evidence that the president's views rest firmly on a foundation of deception layered with a rich mix of confusion and inconsistency is to be found in the enthusiasm with which Britain, China, India, Israel, Australia, Russia, Sweden, Germany, Canada, the Netherlands, Singapore, Korea, South Africa, France and many other nations have launched embryonic stem cell research programs.

The only people who continue to put faith in the policy of promoting government funding for only adult stem cell research that the president is still babbling on about are the president, his close advisors, some conservative groups motivated by deeply-held religious views concerning embryos and a few neoconservative polemicists who seem desperate to find an issue that might bring them redemption after doing such a fine job contributing to the design of American foreign policy under Bush.

Sending a Clear Message

With his veto of the bill creating federal funding and regulation over embryonic stem cell research, the president continues to ask us and, more notably, those who are sick and ailing amongst us, to swallow a false, morally incoherent policy.

Not too long after the president's first speech on the subject, the sick and ailing recognized the president was not wise, but rather wacky, and decided to do something about it. With the help of high-profile efforts involving [President Ronald Reagan's widow] Nancy Reagan, [actors] Christopher Reeve, Mary Tyler Moore, Michael J. Fox and a less visible but incredibly committed and hugely influential phalanx of disease advocacy organizations a sound policy about embryonic stem cell research was articulated.

The policy to permit closely monitored federal funding swung hearts and minds in both houses of Congress. Governors and state legislators and, yes, even those in the media began to understand that the only sensible strategy in the battle against disease, infirmity, disability and death is to put the chips of public funding behind all forms of stem cell research—embryonic and adult.

With his veto the president has now reaffirmed a policy that never made any sense, garnered no scientific support to speak of, was abandoned by both houses of Congress and the leaders of his own party and, most importantly, got no traction with those most in need of the benefits of the research—patients and their families.

The president has now told doctors, researchers and patients to drop dead. Science policy in the Bush administration is best made in the White House, not by scientists and not by Congress.

| "Access to additional stem cell lines will accelerate the potential breakthroughs required to cure . . . a range of diseases afflicting millions of Americans."

The Current Number of Federally Approved Stem Cell Lines Is Inadequate

Juvenile Diabetes Research Foundation International

In the following viewpoint, the Juvenile Diabetes Research Foundation (JDRF) presents the case that American researchers need more embryonic stem cell lines. Such lines, each of which are derived from a single embryo, can be propagated in the laboratory indefinitely. The U.S. stem cell research policy is based on the belief that the number of existing stem cell lines is adequate for research purposes; however, the JDRF contends that there are a number of significant problems with the existing stem cell lines. According to the JDRF, the problems with current stem cell lines are hampering research and necessitate the creation of more stem cell lines. The JDRF is a nonprofit organization that raises money for research in the hope of finding a cure for diabetes.

Juvenile Diabetes Research Foundation International, "Why Federal Stem Cell Policy Must Be Expanded: A JDRF Scientific White Paper," August 2004. Reproduced by permission.

As you read, consider the following questions:

1. What does the author say is the difference between early-passage cells and late-passage cells?
2. What is the basis of JDRF's contention that the existing stem cell lines are not genetically diverse?
3. Why were the NIH-approved stem cell lines cultured with mouse cells, according to the author?

JDRF approaches [the stem cell] issue with a single agenda: to find a cure for type 1 diabetes. Juvenile, or type 1, diabetes afflicts almost two million Americans, many of them children, and strikes tens of thousands more every year at an accelerating rate.

Embryonic stem cell research offers one of the most promising avenues to accomplish JDRF's ultimate goal of a cure. JDRF had hoped that the August 2001 Federal stem cell policy would be the beginning of intense scientific effort to reach this goal. But the objective truth echoed by every leading researcher in the field is that the policy, while well intentioned, will not permit research to advance at the pace it can and must; in fact, the policy is actually *slowing* the scientific progress in Federally funded research that the President himself championed.

As much as anything, the call for an expansion of Federal stem cell policy reflects what scientists have learned since the August 2001 announcement. Our understanding of the science has progressed since then, and knowledge of the NIH [National Institutes of Health]-approved stem cell lines has grown much deeper. It is time to adjust the Federal policy so that it accurately represents the latest understanding of the science. The simple, inescapable fact—acknowledged by the Federal government itself—is that access to additional stem cell lines will accelerate the potential breakthroughs required to cure not only diabetes, but a range of diseases afflicting millions of Americans.

The problems with the existing policy are numerous and pervasive. . . .

Problem One: Only 21 Available Lines

Of the original 78 stem cell derivations that were declared eligible for U.S. federal funding under the August 2001 policy, only 21 are actually available for distribution and study.

Soon after the Bush policy statement, the NIH established the Human Embryonic Stem Cell Registry, listing the human embryonic stem cell lines that met the President's criteria for research to be eligible for Federal funding. The list now includes 78 stem cell derivations. While there is debate among researchers as to whether even 78 lines is an adequate number to create the necessary environment to initiate widespread scientific investigation in the field, the more critical point is that few of those 78 stem cell derivations are, or ever will be, usable for scientists. From a practical standpoint, many of the derivations were in the early phases of development in August of 2001, and have still not been characterized and then expanded so they can be readily available to the research community.

A year after the policy statement was issued, scientists estimated that of more than 70 purported human embryonic stem cell derivations that met the Administration criteria for Federally funded research, only 16 were then available for distribution. Today [in mid-2004], the current NIH Human Embryonic Stem Cell Registry lists just 21 cell lines as being available, including two that have limited availability. The President's vision for developing a Federally funded U.S. stem cell research community was predicated on the immediate and widespread availability of more than 70 stem cell lines; unfortunately, ... less than a third of the lines the Administration thought would be available for research are, in fact, available.

Problem Two: Culture Conditions

Because the NIH-approved stem cell lines were developed using science that has since seen significant improvements and-progress, they may prove to be far more limited in their bio-medical research utility than lines created more recently.

In the development of non-Federally funded stem cell lines [since 2001], there has been continuous improvement in our understanding of the importance of culture conditions. The emerging picture indicates that the culture conditions used to grow human embryonic stem cell lines plays an important role in maintaining cell stability. Research has shown that as stem cell lines are grown in long-term culture, some of them may begin to accumulate chromosomal damage. Implicit in this finding is the suggestion that some older (i.e., late passage) cells can be more susceptible to chromosomal abnormalities than earlier passage cultures.

Unfortunately, some of the stem cell lines available under the Federal policy have no early-passage cells available; researchers can only receive late-passage cells. A number of reports have emerged describing chromosomal abnormalities that have appeared in some NIH-approved stem cell lines after prolonged culture. These reports indicate that among the NIH-approved lines, fewer than the 21 lines may be useful for research or therapies.

Problem Three: Lack of Genetic Diversity

The NIH lines lack the genetic diversity scientists need to do research that could create therapeutic treatments for millions of Americans.

The ability to transplant cells or tissues created from hES [human embryonic stem cell] lines into individuals in order to restore function (insulin-secreting cells for diabetes, dopamine-producing nerve cells for Parkinson's disease, etc.) will depend on overcoming immune system rejection of the transplanted material. Potential recipients of life-saving therapies will come from diverse genetic backgrounds, and it will be more difficult to develop therapeutics from an extremely limited starting population. The limited number of available stem cell lines could have a significant impact in limiting the number of people who might benefit from a transplant using stem cells or tissues derived from stem cells. While perfect HLA [human leukocyte antigen] matches between cells and patients are economically unfeasible, the 21 NIH lines that are currently approved will not represent the genetic diversity required to develop potential therapies for a large number of Americans.

Research in pursuit of a particular goal, such as differentiation of embryonic stem cells into insulin-producing cells, would be accelerated and hold a greater likelihood of success if researchers have the opportunity to study variations in the greatest number of lines, rather than an arbitrary limit that is not based on biologic functional potential. Researchers need to study many lines in order to derive general conclusions, or to develop therapeutics. Expanding the current policy will allow researchers to make important comparisons among stem cell lines.

Problem Four: Lines May Not Be Effective

Because human embryonic stem cells are heterogeneous, with some showing a greater propensity to become certain types of cells, a limited number of stem cell lines can decrease the breadth of research opportunities for scientists.

The number of available lines is particularly important because scientists have learned that some stem cell lines are more effective than others in differentiating to become specific tissues; i.e., some lines may be more effective treating neurological disorders, while others might be more effective treating heart disease or diabetes. This was theorized, but not known in 2001.

Human embryonic stem cells are heterogeneous and diverse, reflecting the fact that each has unique genetic characteristics and differing biological potentials. Clear differences among human embryonic stem cell lines are confirmed by

Federal Guidelines Should Be Loosened

The majority of U.S. citizens, including most physicians, scientists, and ethicists, agree that the U.S. federal guidelines restricting derivation of hESC [human embryonic stem cell] lines should be loosened considerably to allow derivation of new hESC lines from extra embryos generated in the course of IVF [in vitro fertilization] in which the parent-owners consent to having their extra embryos used for research. A compromise might limit and monitor the numbers of such hESC lines that are created. . . . It is important to note that all investigations involving humans involve some risk, and a worthy goal is to minimize these risks without blocking scientific progress.

Civin and Rao, Stem Cells, vol. 24, 2006.

multiple studies that report the characteristics of different cell lines. These functional differences mean that there are also differences in potential to differentiate into various cell types. Some cell lines are more likely to develop into nerve cells, for example, while others are more likely to develop into other tissues. . . .

The limited number of available NIH-approved lines have had difficulty in robustly and reproducibly differentiating the lines to become specific tissues.

Problem Five: Disease-Specific Lines

The absence of disease-specific stem cell lines eligible for federal funding means that the policy is limiting stem cell research on dozens of genetic diseases such as Duchenne muscular dystrophy and Huntinton's disease, potentially adding years to the discovery of treatments for millions of Americans.

Stem cell lines can provide a model system for research to gain a better understanding of the mechanisms underlying a disease, and to develop strategies or drugs designed to treat those illnesses. But because the current Federal policy limits the number of stem cell lines available to researchers using Federal funding, scientists have been limited in their ability to use stem cells to do research on literally dozens of genetic diseases—some rare but others widespread—that impact millions of Americans. An enhanced policy would create broader, more comprehensive, and more beneficial research into dozens of these diseases.

Of the large number of couples who undergo IVF [in vitro fertilization] treatment, some have a family history of various genetic disorders. These couples can use techniques such as pre-implantation genetic diagnosis to identify embryos that are unaffected by those genetic diseases before pregnancy is established. Embryos that are identified in the IVF process as having serious genetic disorders (such as neurofibromatosis, myotonic dystrophy, Fragile X Syndrome, and Fanconi's anemia) are typically not used for fertilization treatment. But such embryos with genetic diseases have been the source for non-Federally funded stem cell lines that have these disease characteristics. Such a stem cell line provides a model system for researchers to gain a better understanding of the mechanisms underlying the disease, and help them to develop strategies or drugs to treat the illness—but cannot be used by scientists accepting NIH funding.

This application is a reality for the disorders listed above—but there are literally dozens of similar genetic diseases that cannot be studied and treated in a similar manner.

Problem Six: Mouse Feeder Cells

All the NIH-approved lines were isolated in contact with mouse "feeder" cells. As a result, the FDA [Food and Drug Administration] must consider any therapies developed using these stem cells as xenotransplants [transplants of tissue from nonhumans], creating a huge hurdle that discourages the biotech and pharmaceutical industries from developing treatments utilizing those lines.

All the NIH-approved stem cell lines were isolated in contact with mouse "feeder" cells, which were required to prevent the uncontrolled differentiation of the embryonic stem cells. Because of the possibility of contamination, treatments could not, under ordinary circumstances, be developed for humans using those stem cell lines. The FDA would consider any therapies developed using these cells to be xenotransplants, requiring clearance of a very high regulatory hurdle before they could be used in humans. For many researchers in academia and industry alike this prospect represents an extraordinary (and expensive) challenge. In comparison, many of the 100 stem cell lines developed since 2001 either do not use feeder cells, or use material that would not present potential xenotransplant issues if eventually transplanted into humans.

Since 2001, scientists have successfully replaced mouse feeders—either with human cells used as feeders, or with feeder-free conditions. Given these advances, forcing researchers to work only with NIH-eligible stem cell lines places arbitrary and unnecessary obstacles to success in the way of possible therapies and treatments. . . .

While each of the . . . supply and quality issues is, in and of itself, a significant reason why the current embryonic stem cell policy needs to be expanded, taken together they create a scientific environment that makes significant discoveries or advances in embryonic stem cell research difficult.

"The kind of basic science being done in the labs . . . is well served by stable, thoroughly characterized lines of stem cells like those funded by the Bush policy."

The Number of Federally Approved Stem Cell Lines Should Not Be Increased

Eric Cohen

In the following viewpoint, Eric Cohen argues that the number of existing federally approved stem cell lines is adequate for American research purposes. He maintains that legislation to expand the number of stem cell lines is not needed and that the vast majority of researchers across the world, even those who have access to other stem cell lines, are using the stable well-characterized lines funded by U.S. policy. Therefore, contends Cohen, there is no need to destroy embryos in order to obtain more stem cell lines. Eric Cohen is the director of the Bioethics and American Democracy program at the Ethics and Public Policy Center in Washington, D.C.

Eric Cohen, "Stem-Cell Sense: Clear Thinking on a Stem Cell Anniversary," *National Review*, May 25, 2006. nationalreview.com. Reproduced by permission.

As you read, consider the following questions:

1. Why are the existing lines called the "Bush stem-cell lines," according to the author?
2. Why does Cohen say that contamination of the existing stem cell lines is no longer a problem?
3. Why does the author say that polling data is misleading?

We are entering a summer of stem-cell anniversaries. August 9 of [2006] will mark the fifth anniversary of President [George W.] Bush's embryonic-stem-cell funding policy, which seeks to support basic stem-cell science without encouraging the ongoing destruction of embryos.

Legislation to Create More Lines

Wednesday [May 24, 2006], meanwhile, marked the first anniversary of the vote in the House of Representatives to overturn President Bush's policy and replace it with one that would encourage the destruction of human embryos for research. On May 24, 2005, the House voted 238-194 in favor of a bill [the U.S. Stem Cell Research Enhancement Act of 2005] sponsored by Representatives Mike Castle and Diana DeGette that would, as the president put it [in 2005], "take us across a critical ethical line by creating new incentives for the ongoing destruction of emerging human life."

Following that vote, Senate action on the bill appeared to be imminent, and it seemed likely that stem cells would be the subject of President Bush's first veto. The momentum for a Senate vote seemed to grow stronger still when Senate Majority Leader Bill Frist announced [in July 2005] that he would support the Castle-DeGette bill. Frist's reversal, the *Washington Post* noted then, "is likely to win over some undecided lawmakers."

Months have passed without a Senate vote, however, and [the May 24, 2006,] *Washington Post* told a very different story. "The political calculus around stem cells has changed in unexpected ways," notes the *Post*. And much of that change, the *Post* adds, has been not political but scientific. The facts on the ground simply don't support the opponents of President Bush's policy.

Flawed Arguments

Before [2005]'s vote, backers of the Castle-DeGette bill generally made four key arguments to persuade lawmakers: (1) that embryonic-stem-cell advances were coming fast and furious, (2) that the stem-cell lines funded by the Bush policy were contaminated and therefore not very useful, (3) that American leadership in the field depended on overturning that policy, and (4) that public support for funding the research was broad and deep.

You still hear these same arguments, but . . . not one of them really holds up to rigorous scrutiny.

The greatest embryonic-stem-cell success that advocates could point to [in 2005] was actually a cloning success—and, as it turns out, was not a success at all. On May 19, 2005, a week before the House voted, Senator Dianne Feinstein released a statement that said:

> The achievements made by scientists in South Korea prove that it is possible to derive patient-specific embryonic stem cell lines using the Somatic Cell Nuclear Transplantation technique. This is a major achievement for the future of regenerative medicine. We are one big step closer to eventually developing treatments for deadly conditions like spinal cord injury and juvenile diabetes. There is no question that this country needs an effective stem cell policy—both to provide federal funding for additional embryonic stem cell lines and to provide federal ethical guidelines.

The "achievements" Feinstein spoke of were, it now turns out, a total fraud. A team of South Korean researchers led by Hwang Woo Suk claimed to have produced cloned human embryos and derived embryonic stem cells from them. [Now] it has been revealed that the researchers' publications were faked, their experiments unsuccessful, and their treatment of egg donors grossly appalling.

In fact, human embryonic-stem-cell research is at a very early stage. There have been no therapeutic applications, or even human trials. Most researchers argue it will be many years before it can be clear whether such applications will be possible. If anything, it now appears they are further behind today than they (thought they) were a year ago. This is not to deny the potential—and potentially unique—value of research using embryonic stem cells. But the excessive hype has long been premature and irresponsible.

Research Well-Served by Existing Lines

The kind of basic science being done in the labs for the moment is well served by stable, thoroughly characterized lines of stem cells like those funded by the Bush policy. In fact, since [the 2005] vote we have learned just how well the so-called "Bush stem-cell lines" have served the needs of researchers. Contrary to the assertions of those who oppose the Bush policy, it turns out the funded stem-cell lines are used in the vast majority of all human embryonic-stem-cell research; a study in the April [2006] issue of *Nature Biotechnology* showed that more than 85 percent of such research around the world has used these lines, and most of it [since 2002]. The $90 million spent by the federal government on such research has surely helped the field, but it is also clear from these figures that many researchers who do not receive NIH [National Institutes of Health] funding are using the Bush stem-cell lines.

What, then, to make of assertions that these lines are contaminated by exposure to animal materials, and therefore useless? That notion, central to the case for the Castle-DeGette bill, has also since fallen apart. A series of articles, including one by stem-cell pioneer James A. Thomson in *Nature Biotechnology*, have shown successful methods of removing ani-

Federally Funded Stem Cell Lines

Listed below are entities that have developed stem cell lines that meet the President's criteria and are therefore eligible for federal funding.

- Bresagen, Inc., Athens Georgia (The cells in line BG04/ hESBGN-04 failed to expand into undifferentiatied cell cultures.)
- Cell & Gene Therapy Research Institute (Pochon CHA University), Seoul, Korea
- Cellartis AB Göteborg, Sweden (Cell line SA03/ Sahlgrenska 3 withdrawn by donor.)
- CyThera, Inc., San Diego, California (The cells failed to expand into undifferentiated cell cultures.)
- ES Cell International Ptd Ld. Singapore
- Geron Corporation, Menlo Park, California
- Göteborg University, Göteborg, Sweden
- Karolinska Institute, Stockholm, Sweden (The cells failed to expand into undifferentiated cell cultures.)
- Maria Biotech Co. Ltd.—Maria Infertility Hospital Medical Institute, Seoul, Korea
- MizMedi Hospital—Seoul National University, Seoul, Korea (Cell line no longer eligible for federal funding.)
- National Centre for Biological Sciences/Tata Institute of Fundamental Research, Bangalore, India
- Reliance Life Sciences, Mumbai, India
- Technion-Israel Institute of Technology, Haifa, Israel
- University of California, San Francisco, California
- Wisconsin Alumni Research Foundation, Madison, Wisconsin

National Institutes of Health, September 2006.

mal materials from the funded lines. Other studies have shown results similar to Thomson's, and the contamination argument has gone the way of the others.

American Research

These technical arguments against the lines were key to the further assertion . . . that the Bush policy was causing America to fall behind other countries in stem-cell research. In her statement praising the Korean research, Senator Feinstein also argued that "federal inaction has created a void that has been only partially filled by states and by private entities, and it has allowed other countries to move ahead of the United States in this important area of cutting-edge medical research."

Even setting aside the fact that some of the research Senator Feinstein was worried about was actually faked, her larger comment about "other countries" moving "ahead of the United States" was totally wrong. The same *Nature Biotechnology* study that showed how widely the NIH-funded lines are used also showed that American scientists are by far the world leaders in embryonic-stem-cell research—publishing 46 percent of all articles on the subject, with the remainder divided among 17 other countries. American publications in the field have been growing each year (from 3 in 2002 to 20 in 2004). Publications around the world have also been accelerating, of course, but no single country comes close to America's dominant position.

Most Americans Oppose Funding More Lines

The Castle-DeGette bill's backers have just one card left: public opinion. Even if none of their arguments hold up, they claim that they have persuaded the public, and that this is reason enough to change the policy. But even this claim doesn't hold up.

Castle-DeGette supporters, [the] *Post* notes, "point to new polling data indicating that a greater majority of Americans than ever, 72 percent, support the research—a finding that candidates, they say, cannot afford to ignore."

But note how the poll they cite actually frames the issue:

Embryonic stem cells are special cells that can develop into every type of cell in the human body. The stem cells are extracted from embryonic cells produced in fertility clinics and then frozen days after fertilization. If a couple decides that the fertilized eggs are no longer needed, they can choose to donate the embryos for research or the clinic will throw the embryos away. Scientists have had success in initial research with embryonic stem cells and believe that they can be developed into cures for diseases such as cancer, Parkinson's, heart disease, juvenile diabetes, and spinal cord injuries.

Those being questioned are given a vastly exaggerated impression of the promise of the science. And they are never told the research involves the destruction of human embryos—in fact, the way the poll frames the issue almost suggests the research is an alternative to the destruction of embryos.

Moreover, they are not then asked what they think of the current federal policy, or whether it should be changed. They are not told that the government already funds this research, and funds it in ways that do not encourage the further destruction of embryos. Instead, they are asked: "Having heard this description, do you strongly favor, somewhat favor, somewhat oppose, or strongly oppose medical research that uses stem cells from human embryos?" Forty-two percent say they strongly favor it, while another 30 percent "somewhat favor" the research.

Given his funding policy, it may well be that President Bush himself would be among that 72 percent of supporters—after all, he was the first president to fund the research, even if within moral limits.

Very few polls actually ask the public for views on the existing funding policy, rather than general impressions about stem-cell research. And those that do find a rather different picture than the one portrayed by advocates of embryo-destroying research. [One] of these polls was actually done just at the time the supporters of the Castle-DeGette bill were making their case most fervently and publicly, the very week the House [in 2005]. As the House was preparing to vote (with many congressmen operating on the assumption that a vast majority of the country supported overturning the Bush policy), this poll found that only 37 percent of those questioned actually wanted to fund more stem-cell lines. In other words, support for embryonic stem-cell research does not necessarily translate into support for a federal funding policy that promotes and pays for the ongoing destruction of human embryos.

Policy Successful

[In 2006], very little remains of the arguments that seemed so persuasive then. On the contrary, developments in techniques to derive embryonic-like stem cells without requiring the destruction of embryos have given new ammunition to supporters of the current policy. The momentum has shifted firmly against the Castle-DeGette bill, even if most advocates continue to spout the same arguments, and many in the press continue to parrot them.

What this will mean politically remains an open question. But it is undeniable that much has happened in the field of stem-cell research . . . that should make Senators look at the Castle-DeGette bill in a new light, and better appreciate the Bush policy's successful effort to balance science and ethics.

"In general, 72 percent [of Americans]
support expanded federal government
support for medical research, including
stem cell research."

Americans Favor Government Support of Human Embryonic Stem Cell Research

Civil Society Institute/Results for America

In the following viewpoint, presented by the Results for America project of the Civil Society Institute, Americans are found to favor embryonic stem cell research. According to the Civil Society Institute, public support for federally funded embryonic stem cell research is rising and politicians at both the state and federal levels should take notice. The Civil Society Institute is an independent nonprofit organization dedicated to supporting and encouraging the involvement of community-level groups and individuals in the public life of the country.

As you read, consider the following questions:

1. According to the Civil Society Institute, what is behind the rise in public support for federal funding of embryonic stem cell research?

Civil Society Institute/Results for America, "Survey: More Americans Support Stem Cell Research, with Even Wider Backing Seen for Bipartisan Federal Bill, State Pushes," Civil Society Institute, February 15, 2005. www.resultsforamerica.org. Reproduced by permission.

2. What happens to the level of support for embryonic stem cell research when an explanation of the research is provided, according to the author?

3. According to the author, what percentage of respondents do or might support state-level stem cell initiatives?

More than three out of five Americans (63 percent) back embryonic stem cell research, and even higher levels of support exist for bipartisan federal legislation to promote more such research (70 percent) and the growing number of state-level initiatives to encourage stem cell work (76 percent do or might support such measures), according to a new survey conducted by Opinion Research Corporation (ORC) on behalf of the Results for America (RFA) project of the nonprofit and nonpartisan Civil Society Institute.

Reagan's Death, Contaminated Lines Spur Support

On the eve of the introduction of [the U.S. Stem Cell Research Enhancement Act of 2005] in Congress by Rep. Michael Castle and Rep. Diana DeGette to expand federal stem cell research, the RFA survey shows that a growing number of Americans favor going beyond President George W. Bush's strict limits on stem cell research for medical research purposes. The level of public support for wider federal stem cell research now is slightly higher than it was after the death of former President Ronald Reagan, whose widow, Nancy Reagan, called for the elimination of barriers to the exploration of stem cells for possible medical treatments.

Another factor identified by the survey as driving the public's support for stem cell research: The recent announcement that most or all of the stem cell lines approved for federal research purposes have been compromised, and thereby rendered useless for the pursuit of possible medical cures.

Civil Society Institute President Pam Solo said: "These findings clearly show that stem cell research is not an issue

Using Poll Results

Few science and technology–related issues have sparked as much survey attention as the public controversy over human embryonic stem cell research and therapeutic cloning. Interest groups, advocates, and policymakers on both sides of the debate have taken advantage of poll results to support their claims that the public backs their preferred policy outcomes, and the competing camps have staged ongoing public communication campaigns in an effort to shape public opinion. Journalists have also highlighted the results of these surveys, using poll figures to complement their coverage of who is ahead and who is behind in the competition to decide stem cell–and cloning-related policy.

Matthew Nisbet, Dominique Brossard, and Adrienne Kroepsch,
Harvard International Journal of Press/Politics, 8(2), 2003.

that is going to go away. If anything, the level of public backing is rising, edging up from the high-water mark of support brought about by the extensive public discussion about stem cell research in the wake of the passing of former President Ronald Reagan. The growing number of state-level ballot initiatives and legislative pushes means that federal lawmakers have two choices: either get out front and lead on this issue or be overtaken by all of the clamoring for stem cell research that is bubbling up from the grassroots level."

High Level of Support

ORC Senior Project Manager Graham Hueber said: "The very high level of support for the proposed bipartisan federal legislation on stem cell research is quite striking in these findings. Respondents in higher income households (77 percent) and those with a college degree (76 percent) are significantly more likely to support the bill than those with lower levels of education or income. And while liberals are very much in support of the legislation (86 percent), so, too, are most moderates (80 percent) and more than half of conservatives. What we see in these numbers is that the bipartisan approach to addressing the stem cell issue takes what is already a strong overall level of support and makes it even stronger."

In August 2001, the Bush administration imposed a major new restriction on federal funding for embryonic stem cell research. The restriction meant that research on stem cell lines created before August 2001 could receive funding, but prohibited support for research on stem cell lines developed after that date.

Key Survey Findings

- Support for embryonic stem cell research continues to grow, with 63 percent of American adults now supporting it and 28 percent in opposition—and only 17 percent terming themselves "strongly opposed." These unaided findings compare favorably with the June 2004 RFA survey in the wake of the death of President Ronald Reagan, when stem cell research support climbed to 60 percent–26 percent. The same question posed in 2001 found support at 48 percent–43 percent. When an explanation is provided of embryonic stem cell research, the support level rises to 72 percent–25 percent, including 55 percent of conservatives. This was roughly unchanged from the June 2004 survey, when the margin was 72 percent–23 percent.

- Amidst reports that the stem cells lines approved by President Bush for research purposes have been contaminated and rendered unusable, 69 percent support "expanding President Bush's policy in this area to allow federal funding for research on stem cells developed from excess embryos frozen in fertil-

163

ity clinics and donated by the parents." This level of support includes 56 percent of conservatives, with 80 percent of moderates and 84 percent of liberals.

- Support for the bipartisan stem cell research . . . introduced by Rep. Castle, R-DE., and Rep. Diana DeGette, D-CO., is strong at 70 percent–26 percent, including 53 percent of conservatives, 80 percent of moderates and 86 percent of liberals. The bill would expand federal funding for research on stem cells that are developed from embryos frozen in fertility clinics and which otherwise would be discarded.

- More than three out of four (76 percent) do or might support state-level stem cell initiatives, with 21 percent in opposition. Of the first number, 58 percent said "yes" and 18 percent indicated they might support such state-level pushes.

- In general, 72 percent support expanded federal government support for medical research, including stem cell research.

- Over half (54 percent) are or might be concerned about a stem cell "brain drain" with U.S. researchers going overseas, with 42 percent not being concerned. Of the first number, 38 percent indicated they are concerned and 16 percent indicated they might be concerned.

| "Most Americans do not support feder-
ally funded research that requires destroying human embryos."

Americans Do Not Favor Government Support of Human Embryonic Stem Cell Research

United States Conference of Catholic Bishops

In the following viewpoint, the United States Conference of Catholic Bishops (USCCB) contends that most Americans oppose embryonic stem cell research that destroys embryos and that an overwhelming number of Americans oppose the use of human cloning to create embryos for use in stem cell research. The US-CCB is the official governing body of the Roman Catholic Church in the United States.

As you read, consider the following questions:

1. According to the USCCB poll, what percentage of Americans oppose federal funding of stem cell research that destroys human embryos?

United States Conference of Catholic Bishops, "New Poll: Americans Continue to Oppose Funding Stem Cell Research that Destroys Human Embryos," May 31, 2006. Reproduced by permission.

165

2. What does the poll show about Americans' support of human cloning?

3. What type of stem cell research do the authors say most American's support the funding of?

A [2006] poll shows that 48% of Americans oppose federal funding of stem cell research that requires destroying human embryos, while only 39% support such funding. The poll, conducted by International Communications Research (ICR), surveyed over one thousand adults by telephone May 19–23, 2006.

Legislation to fund such embryonic stem cell research [the Stem Cell Research Enhancement Act of 2005], approved by the U.S. House of Representatives . . . , may soon be considered in the Senate. [The poll] was commissioned by the Secretariat for Pro-Life Activities of the U.S. Conference of Catholic Bishops (USCCB).

When survey respondents were informed that scientists disagree on whether stem cells from embryos or from adult tissues and other alternative sources may end up being most successful in treating diseases, 57% favored funding only the research avenues that do not harm the donor; only 24% favored funding all stem cell research, including the type that involves destroying embryos.

Most Americans Oppose Embryo Research and Cloning

"Congress should not be misled on this important issue," said Richard M. Doerflinger, Deputy Director of the USCCB's Secretariat for Pro-Life Activities. "Most Americans do not support federally funded research that requires destroying human embryos. Our opponents also know this. No doubt this is why their public statements—and many of their own opinion polls—either ignore or misrepresent what this research involves, while irresponsibly hyping its potential for miracle cures."

Moral Evaluations of Stem Cell Research

Much of the opposition to embryonic stem cell research from religious and conservative elites derives from the necessary destruction of human embryos. At the base of this elite opposition is the belief that a human embryo is equivalent to a human life, and that embryos are deserving of the same protections as other human beings. To destroy embryos would therefore be morally wrong, essentially equivalent to murder. Where does the public weigh in on this matter? Previous surveys that have asked Americans about when life begins indicate that a slight majority of respondents have consistently indicated that life begins at "conception."

Matthew Nisbet, Committee for the Scientific Investigation of Claims of the Paranormal, May 2, 2004.

The [2006] poll also shows overwhelming opposition to human cloning, whether to provide children for infertile couples (83% against) or to produce embryos that would be destroyed in medical research (81% against).

A comparison with identical polls conducted by ICR in 2004 and 2005 shows a fairly consistent level of moral concern on this issue on the part of the American public. Federally funded embryonic stem cell research has never garnered majority support in this poll, reaching a high of 43% in August 2004. For the third year in a row, when informed of their options, most Americans support funding only stem cell research that does not require destroying embryos.

The ICR polls also consistently show opposition of 77% or higher to human cloning, whether for reproduction or medical research. The poll's figure of 81% opposed to cloning human embryos for research is the highest in three years.

Questions asked by International Communications Research, a national research firm headquartered in Media, Pennsylvania (a weighted sample of 1022 American adults was surveyed by telephone May 19–23, 2006, with a margin of error of plus or minus 3.1 percent):

1. Stem cells are the basic cells from which all of a person's tissues and organs develop. Congress is considering the question of federal funding for experiments using stem cells from human embryos. The live embryos would be destroyed in their first week of development to obtain these cells. Do you support or oppose using your federal tax dollars for such experiments?

Support	38.6%
Oppose	47.8%
Don't know	11.9%
Refused	1.7%

2. Stem cells for research can be obtained by destroying human embryos. They can also be obtained from adults, from placentas left over from live births, and in other ways that do no harm to the donor. Scientists disagree on which source may end up being most successful in treating diseases. How would you prefer your tax dollars to be used this year for stem cell research?

(Options rotated)

Supporting all methods, including those that require destroying human embryos, to see which will be most successful	23.6%
Supporting research using adult stem cells andother alternatives, to see if there is no need to destroy human embryos for research	56.8%
Neither (volunteered)	11.1%
Don't know	7.2%
Refused	1.3%

3. Should scientists be allowed to use human cloning to try to create children for infertile couples?

Yes	9.7%
No	83.4%
Don't know	5.9%
Refused	1.0%

4. Should scientists be allowed to use human cloning to create a supply of human embryos to be destroyed in medical research?

Yes	11.4%
No	81.2%
Don't know	6.6%
Refused	0.8%

"It has become clear to American scientists that [U.S. stem cell research] policy has put them at a disadvantage compared with many of their colleagues overseas."

U.S. Policy Is Hurting Stem Cell Research in the United States

Gareth Cook

In the following viewpoint, Gareth Cook contends that the restrictions on embryonic stem cell research in the United States are causing many scientists to seek research positions overseas and are enabling other countries to emerge as powerhouses in the stem cell research field. The U.S. policy outlined by President George W. Bush in 2001 restricts the number of stem cell lines that federally funded American researchers can use. According to Cook, this restriction is hampering American research. Gareth Cook, a reporter for the Boston Globe, *was awarded the 2005 Pulitzer Prize for Explanatory Journalism for his reports on stem cell research.*

Gareth Cook, "U.S. Stem Cell Research Lagging: Without Aid, Work Moving Overseas," *Boston Globe*, May 23, 2004. Copyright © 2004 Globe Newspaper Company. Republished with permission of the *Boston Globe*, conveyed through Copyright Clearance Center, Inc.

As you read, consider the following questions:

1. Where specifically was the first human embryonic stem cell line created, according to Cook?
2. According to the author, what is a stem cell line?
3. According to Cook, because of the U.S. policy, embryonic stem cell research in the United States is increasingly being funded by what two sources?

L ast spring [in 2003], [Czech] biologist Petr Dvorak's cellphone rang with the news that his lab, a simple cement building not far from the rolling farmland of Moravia, had just entered the forefront of global science.

He rushed to work, down a cracked blacktop walkway and past a sagging barbed-wire fence. Then Dvorak, 48, peered through a microscope and saw what had triggered the call: He and his team had isolated a new line of human embryonic stem cells.

"We were so happy," said Dvorak, who is a member of the Czech Academy of Sciences. "I couldn't sleep for a week."

Most New Lines Are Created Overseas

Although the first human embryonic stem cell line was created in the United States, a *Globe* survey has found that the majority of new embryonic cell lines—colonies of potent cells with the ability to create any type of tissue in the human body—are now being created overseas, a concrete sign that American science is losing its preeminence in a key field of 21st-century research.

[In 2001], the [George W.] Bush administration prohibited the use of federal money to work with any embryonic cell lines created after Aug. 9, 2001, because of moral concerns over the destruction of human embryos. At the time, the president said there would be more than 60 lines of these cells available. But today there are only 19 usable lines created before that date, and that number is never likely to rise above 23, according to the National Institutes of Health [NIH].

However, the number of cell lines available to the world's researchers, but off-limits to US government-funded researchers, is now much higher: at least 51, according to the survey. It could rise to more than 100 [by mid-2005]. There are three new lines in Dvorak's lab, with four more in progress. And there are also new lines in Sweden, Israel, Finland, and South Korea. [In May 2004], the world's first public bank of embryonic stem cells opened in the United Kingdom, a country where there are at least five new lines and more on the way.

"Science is like a stream of water, because it finds its way," said Susan Fisher, a professor at the University of California at San Francisco. "And now it has found its way outside the United States."

America Is Losing Dominance

At a time when reports show the United States is losing its dominance in other areas of science, Fisher and many other researchers say they are increasingly worried that America is not building a competitive foundation in one of the most active areas of biological discovery. Many scientists believe that embryonic stem-cell research has the potential to yield profound insights into a range of afflictions, including Parkinson's disease and diabetes, which affect millions of Americans. By restricting American use of these cells, they say, the government is effectively keeping them out of the hands of many top scientists—both slowing the pace of research that could lead to cures, and potentially putting the country behind in technologies that could be major business opportunities in the new century.

Included on the list of off-limits cell lines created since 2001 are some cells that are easier to use and would be safer for patients than the Bush-approved lines. Others are tailored for the study of particular diseases.

Each cell line is a colony of cells derived from a single embryo, which share the same DNA. One of the new cell lines has the common genetic mutation underlying cystic fibrosis. This cell line, developed overseas and not yet described in a scientific journal, could reveal the biological underpinnings of a debilitating disease that affects some 30,000 Americans. The US government will not pay for scientists to grow or study these cells because they were created recently.

U.S. Government Restrictions

The ballooning list of forbidden cell lines could add energy to a rebellion over stem cell policy within the president's own Republican Party. Thirty-six Republicans were among the 206 members of the House of Representatives who signed a letter asking the president to reconsider the ban. [In 2004], Nancy Reagan delivered an impassioned plea for research that might one day prevent the horror of diseases like Alzheimer's, which she said ha[d] taken former president Ronald Reagan "to a distant place where I c[ould] no longer reach him."

For most diseases, embryonic stem cell research is likely many years from offering any help to patients. But it is becoming increasingly apparent that if researchers begin to make medical progress, the US government—which funds the vast majority of basic science research in this country—will be able to take little credit.

For many foreign scientists, the restrictions imposed on the world's leading biomedical power represent an opportunity. Dvorak once used old rum bottles as flasks in his underfunded lab. Now he is talking to a professor at Harvard Medical School, Dr. Ole Isacson, about collaborating on research.

"He is swimming," said Isacson, whose lab at McLean Hospital is famous for its research on Parkinson's disease. "But for us, it is like trying to swim on dry land."

When human embryonic stem cells were first isolated, the breakthrough happened in an American lab.

In November 1998, a team of researchers lead by biologist James Thomson of the University of Wisconsin–Madison announced it had isolated human embryonic stem cells and could grow them in a dish. Embryonic stem cells, taken from a microscopic embryo in its first few days of development, are in a sense the most primordial and powerful human cells, and can develop into any part of the body.

The announcement created a sensation. It was clear these cells would be an important new tool for studying human biology, and they also raised the prospect that a wide range of diseases might be treated someday by replacing a patient's damaged cells. Yet the work is also ethically controversial, because growing stem cells requires destroying a human embryo. This led critics to charge the practice amounted to taking human lives and could not be justified no matter how great the potential benefits.

In 2001, President Bush attempted to broker a compromise: In a nationally televised speech, he said that federally funded research would be limited to cell lines already in existence. He said that the more than 60 lines already derived would be enough for researchers to continue their work without using government money to destroy more embryos.

Although much basic biological research remains to be done on the cell lines created before Aug. 9, 2001, it has become clear to American scientists that the Bush policy has put them at a disadvantage compared with many of their colleagues overseas. Human embryonic stem cells are notoriously difficult to handle, and deriving each new line gives the team in the laboratory a deeper understanding of stem-cell biology and essential practical skills. Abroad, this work is exploding, while in the United States only a handful of labs are able to do it.

"A lot of stem cell biology is like gardening," said Stephen Minger, who isolated the cystic fibrosis cell line and is an

Controversy Surrounds hES Research

In the United States, federal debates about funding for research involving new hES [human embryonic stem] cell lines have been delayed. . . . Legal challenges to the largest state-initiated hES cell funding program are proceeding slowly through the courts. While policy makers struggle to define a stable, politically and scientifically tenable approach to supporting basic hES cell research, a high-profile case of fraud has led to the retraction of two of the field's breakthrough papers. Today's combination of scientific and political turmoil further exacerbates worries about the legitimacy, potential and future of hES cell research.

Jason Owen-Smith and Jennifer McCormick,
Nature Biotechnology, April 2006.

American scientist who now works at King's College London. "Some people can grow orchids, and some can't grow tomatoes."

Research Occurring in Other Countries

Governments around the world are stepping into the gap, and a number are emerging as powerhouses in the field.

In the United Kingdom, as in the United States, there has been contentious public debate over embryonic cell research, but the government has designed a system of strict oversight. With the opening [in May 2004] of the new UK Stem Cell Bank north of London, funded by the government at $4.6 million over three years, that country is taking the kind of international leadership role which in other fields has fallen to the United States. The bank will accept cell lines that meet a set of ethical standards, carefully study and grow them to ensure they are scientifically useful, and then make them available to researchers.

"We see this as a truly international effort," said Glyn Stacey, the bank's director.

In Australia, the government is funding research and helping to set up a national stem cell center. In the Czech Republic, Dvorak's lab at the Mendel University of Agriculture and Forestry is part of a Centre for Cell Therapy and Tissue Repair, supported by the government. South Korea has derived almost as many new lines of human embryonic stem cells as the United States, according to the *Globe* survey, and researchers there were the first to create stem cells from a cloned human embryo—a scientific milestone that American researchers grumble should have happened in the United States.

This rush of work overseas is yielding other important advances, such as technology that could be key in turning the science of embryonic stem cells into usable therapies. All of the cell lines on the US government approved list are grown on a layer of mouse cells. These mouse cells, called a "feeder layer," sustain the human cells, but could also transmit mouse-borne viruses, making them potentially dangerous for use in humans.

Dvorak's laboratory has just begun working with human feeder cells instead, a technique that could yield cells safe to transplant back into humans. Already, laboratories in Singapore, Israel, Sweden, and Finland have isolated lines of stem cells that don't need mouse feeder cells. Only one American lab has done so: Susan Fisher's California lab, which is barred from receiving federal funding and is supported in part by the California-based biotech Geron Corp.

Private Funding and State Initiatives

None of these lines, including Fisher's, can be used by government-funded scientists in America. The result is that American scientists with private funding are making advances that they can share freely with scientists overseas, but which they cannot share with colleagues in their own departments.

As much as the Bush rules have limited embryonic stem cell research, they have prompted a substantial private effort to keep the research moving forward. Harvard announced [in April 2004] that it [was] building a privately funded effort to do the work, and it ha[d] a fund-raising goal of $100 million. The University of California, San Francisco is already underway with a similar effort, started with a $5 million gift from Intel's Andy Grove, as are a number of other academic institutions. [In May 2004], the governor of New Jersey signed an agreement opening the nation's first state-funded stem cell institute.

Thanks partly to this effort, none of the researchers contacted by the *Globe* said they had seen signs of a scientific "brain drain" that some critics predicted. But still they worry about the more subtle side effects of the Bush policy. Many of the world's top disease specialists work at universities in the United States, yet they are largely unable to work on embryonic stem cells, and the universities are likely to have more trouble recruiting talented foreign scientists interested in embryonic stem cells.

Where Will Young American Scientists Work?

At the same time, top American researchers who might otherwise jump into the field are avoiding it because of the risks, scientists said. And some worry that younger stem cell scientists, who don't have an established lab to keep them in the United States, will move abroad, and perhaps stay there.

"That is really something to keep an eye on," said John Gearhart, one of the field's founders and a professor at Johns Hopkins Medicine. Gearhart said that many of the younger scientists in his lab are interested in pursuing further training abroad.

Yet there could be changes coming. [In May 2004], the NIH issued a letter hinting the White House may be open to changing its policy at some point. The letter, written by NIH director Dr. Elias A. Zerhouni, was a response to a letter signed by 206 members of the House of Representatives. In it, he acknowledges that "from a purely scientific perspective more cell lines may well speed some areas of human embryonic stem cell research."

US Representative Michael N. Castle, a Delaware Republican who helped organize the House letter, said that it seems to represent a softening of the White House stance. In Congress, he said, support for stem cell research is increasing, and he added that he has been struck by the degree to which some people change their minds when they meet with patients who are suffering. "There doesn't seem to be a lot of gray area," Castle said. "They become real advocates."

In the meantime, many scientists abroad are nearly giddy with the possibilities the field now presents them. Dvorak and a colleague, Ales Hampl, are preparing to come to Boston for a major conference . . . , organized by the International Society for Stem Cell Research. While he is in Boston, Dvorak is going to make a presentation of his work at Isacson's lab.

Because of federal restrictions in the United States, Isacson said that he has been increasingly looking abroad for collaborators who are more free, and Dvorak is one possibility.

Sitting in his modest Czech office, next to a fax machine that doubles as his phone, Dvorak said that he is nervous about presenting at Harvard, and has already had nightmares. After many years of laboring in obscurity, a collaboration with Harvard would be a vindication for him, but he struggles to find the words in English.

"It would be like being in heaven," suggested Hampl.

"Yes," said Dvorak, "like being in heaven."

| "*Despite its so-called 'restrictive' policies, the U.S. remains the world's leader in the field of stem cell research.*"

U.S. Policy Is Not Hurting Stem Cell Research in the United States

Do No Harm: The Coalition of Americans for Research Ethics

In the following viewpoint, the Do No Harm coalition disputes evidence that shows the United States falling behind the rest of the world in stem cell research. According to the organization, proponents of human embryonic stem cell research are distorting the results of studies that analyzed the vibrancy of stem cell research in the United States compared with other countries. In fact, the organization argues, the evidence actually shows that the United States is leading the way in embryonic stem cell research. Do No Harm: The Coalition of Americans for Research Ethics seeks to advance medical therapies that do not involve the destruction of embryos.

Do No Harm: The Coalition of Americans for Research Ethics, "'Falling Behind' in Stem Cell Research?: Embryonic Stem Cell Research Proponents Misrepresent Recent Findings," May 2006. Reproduced by permission.

As you read, consider the following questions:

1. In the study published in the *Scientist*, and cited by Do No Harm, what were the two different rankings that were used regarding published stem cell articles?
2. Which two countries have the most "restrictive" policies on stem cell research, according to the author?
3. According to Do No Harm, what percentage of human embryonic stem cell research worldwide depended on U.S. approved stem cell lines?

Is the United States "falling behind" the rest of the world in stem cell research?

Proponents of human embryonic stem cell research (hESCR) say yes, and blame it on current federal policy limiting the number of human embryonic stem cell lines available for federally funded research.

But where is the evidence that the U.S. is actually "falling behind" the rest of the world in stem cell research? Proponents of hESCR point to recent studies they say prove their point. But despite their spinning, the studies show no such thing. In fact, they show just the opposite—that despite its so-called "restrictive" policies, the U.S. remains the world's leader in the field of stem cell research.

Studies Distorted

For example, a [2006] survey conducted in Germany attempted to rank nations by the number of stem cell articles published in scientific journals on a per capita basis. The study found that Israel ranked first, with the U.S. far behind at number six. *The Scientist* (3/21/06), for example, trumpeted this finding in its lead paragraph reporting on the survey.

But as a measure of leadership in any given field of research, the number of articles published per capita is a virtually meaningless statistic. The statistic may show that Israel is a small country with a small but very well educated population. Or does it perhaps show that the U.S. is a large country with a large number of people, many of whom have chosen to do things other than stem cell research? So what?

The really key finding of the survey does not come until the fifth paragraph (out of eight) of *The Scientist* report: that the U.S. is by far the world's leader in the total number of stem cell articles published, alone accounting for 42% of all stem cell articles published worldwide between 2000 and 2004—even with its supposedly restrictive approach to stem cell research. That is four times the articles published by the second leading nation, Germany, which accounted for 10.2% of all stem cell articles published worldwide. Germany, by the way, has the most restrictive policies governing hESCR in all Europe, and led other European nations in the number of articles published.

So the data show that the two nations with more "restrictive" policies on stem cell research lead the world in the number of stem cell papers published.

Even more egregious than the distortions of this study, were those that accompanied one done by researchers at Stanford and published in *Nature Biotechnology*, "An international gap in human ES cell research."

A press release accompanying the study noted that one of its co-authors "said the paper doesn't necessarily prove that federal policies are holding back human embryonic stem cell research." Nonetheless, the *Washington Post*'s story about the study flatly stated, "American scientists are falling behind researchers elsewhere in stem cell discoveries *because of U.S. limits on the use of federal funding, a study has found*" (emphasis added).

Although the Stanford authors could not claim this outright, they nonetheless do their best to "interpret" the data to show that "US congressional delays and the Bush administration's resistance to an expansion of federal funding suggest a real danger for US biomedicine. . . ."

Other Countries Are More Restrictive

Now it appears that, even hobbled by federal funding restrictions, the United States is still leading the world in the stem cell research race. America's Christian right garners a tremendous amount of attention at home for its opposition to stem cell research, yet major portions of Europe have adopted policies far more restrictive than those in the United States. And, despite some impressive breakthroughs in Asia, limited access to private funds and global research networks keeps that region from sprinting ahead of the field. The United States may be the leader in this biomedical research race, but for that it has the rest of the world to thank.

Robert L. Paarlberg,
Foreign Policy, *May/June 2005.*

Evidence Shows Something Different

But the evidence they cite would seem to show something very different:

- The United States remains the world's leader in number of published stem cell articles generally, *and* human embryonic stem cell articles specifically.

- From 1998 (when the field began) through the end of 2004, the United States alone published 46% of all papers published worldwide on hESCR—by far the single largest portion. The remaining 54 percent was divided among 17 other countries. (By comparison with the German study, note that the U.S. share of ESC articles is an even bigger percentage of the whole than its share of stem cell articles generally).

- The number of papers published by the U.S. has been increasing annually.

- Eighty-five percent of all human embryonic stem cell research published through the end of 2004 used the lines eligible for federal funding in the U.S.—that includes *all* published research, both in the U.S. *and overseas.*

(Because researchers abroad are not subject to the "limitations" of U.S. federal funding policy and they do not apply for or receive NIH [National Institutes of Health] funds, it appears they use the supposedly "worthless" and "outdated" federally approved human embryonic stem cell lines because the lines are valuable for research, not because funding limits force them to use them).

So where is the author's evidence that the U.S. is falling behind internationally in hESCR?

The best they can do is note that in 2002, the U.S. accounted for a third of all hESCR papers published (3 out of 10) while by 2004, the U.S. share had dropped to one quarter of all papers published (20 out of 77). Thus the title of their paper: "An international gap in human ES cell research."

But the real "gap" is that no country in the world is anywhere near catching up with the U.S.

The numbers show that between 2002 and 2004, the U.S. produced a seven-fold increase in the total number of papers it published. For all other countries *combined*, there was an eight-fold increase. This hardly seems to prove "a storm is brewing for [U.S.] stem cell science," as the authors contend.

Remember that the authors are comparing U.S. publication with publication by all other nations combined. The fact remains, however, that the U.S. continues to be, by far, the single largest publisher of papers on stem cell research, and that is not likely to change.

Like so much in the area of embryonic stem cell research, the assertion that current federal policy on hESCR is causing the U.S. to become the international class dunce in this field is another myth we are expected to believe for no other reason than that the so-called experts repeat it over and over.

Of course, the U.S. remains tied with all other nations in the world in studies showing a *human treatment* from human ESCs. Since 1998, that number has remained steady at zero.

Periodical Bibliography

The following articles have been selected to supplement the diverse views presented in this chapter.

BBS News   "Right Wing Distortions and Falsehoods on Stem Cells," bbsnews.net, July 20, 2006. www.bbsnews.net.

Tom Coburn   "Stem-Cell Bill Rests on 'False Hope,'" *Hill*, August 23, 2006.

David DeGrazia   "Moral Status, Human Dignity, and Early Embryos: A Critique of the President's Approach," *Journal of Law and Medical Ethics*, Spring 2006.

Theodore Dana Hall "The Stem Cell Controversy—Connecting the Dots," *Bleeping Herald*, March 16, 2006.

Tom Harkin and   "Remarks at the Center for American Progress
Jim Doyle   on Stem Cell Research," *Political Transcript Wire*, August 4, 2006.

Thomas Lang   "Getting Right on Stem Cell Legislation," *CJR Daily*, May 24, 2006. www.cjrdaily.org.

Aaron D. Levine   "Research Policy and the Mobility of U.S. Stem Cell Scientists," *Nature Biotechnology*, July 2006.

Mahendra S. Rao   "Embryonic Stem Cell Research and U.S. Policy," *Stem Cells*, September 6, 2006.

Byron J. Richards   "Bush's Stem Cell Propaganda," *NewsWithViews.com*, July 20, 2006. www.newswithviews .com.

Jessie Ron   "The Promise of Tomorrow: Despite the Controversy That Surrounds Stem Cell Research, Those in the Field Believe the Future Is Bright," *New Scientist*, June 24, 2006.

Arlen Specter   "Senator Specter Speaks on the Senate Floor Regarding Stem Cell Research," July 16, 2006. http://specter.senate.gov.

OPPOSING
VIEWPOINTS®
SERIES

CHAPTER 4

Are There Alternatives to Embryonic Stem Cells?

Chapter Preface

When James Thomson discovered a way to extract and culture human embryonic stem cells, he and the University of Wisconsin (under the auspices of the Wisconsin Alumni Research Foundation [WARF]) applied for and were granted two broad patents by the U.S. Patent Office, one for the embryonic stem cells and one for the techniques he used to extract and grow the stem cells. Some scientists and organizations think that the patents on human embryonic stem cells held by Thomson and WARF should not have been granted. Additionally, they believe the patents are too broad and are impeding stem cell research.

Several groups are challenging the stem cell patents because, they argue, the method used by Thomson to grow the embryonic stem cells was already "invented." In July 2006, the Foundation for Taxpayer and Consumer Rights and the Public Patent Foundation filed a request to the U.S. Patent Office to invalidate the Thomson patent, contending that earlier work by other scientists had made the work done in Wisconsin obvious and not patentable. To receive a patent, an invention must be new, useful, and unobvious. They maintain that the techniques Thomson used to grow his human embryonic stem cells were developed prior to 1998, but in other species such as mice and pigs. All Thomson did, they argue, is to apply those same techniques to humans. In an interview with the *Scientist* magazine, Carl Gulbrandsen of WARF maintained that it is "ludicrous to suggest that the discovery was obvious. It certainly was novel and was considered by *Science* as being the discovery of the year and was on the cover of *Time* magazine."

There is also a contention that WARF and Thomson's patents are so broad and restrictive that they are hampering the progress of stem cell research. The patents give Thomson and

WARF control over every human embryonic stem cell line made in the United States. As John Simpson from the Foundation for Taxpayers and Consumer Rights commented, "These patents cover not only the way James Thomson isolated stem cells, but the very cells themselves. Patenting embryonic stem cells because you have a method to isolate them is like patenting chickens because you have a new method to provide chickenfeed. Or, like patenting food because you can cook."

Contentions that the patents are restrictive stem from the way WARF charges to use the cells. Academic and nonprofit scientists pay $500 to obtain the cells and can study them free of charge. But commercial entities pay fees ranging from $25,000 to $2 million in up-front costs with royalties and thousands of dollars in annual maintenance fees tacked on. Dr. Robert Goldstein, chief scientific officer for the Juvenile Diabetes Research Foundation, has stated that the patents are "a major inhibition to productive scientific research." But Beth Donley, executive director of the WiCell Research Insitute, a subsidiary of WARF, takes issue with these claims, asserting that "WARF created WiCell to support stem cell researchers and has provided free licenses and cells to 324 research groups. WARF believes the Thomson patents are valid and will affirm the validity of the patents."

WARF and Thomson stand to make millions, if not billions, in royalties if embryonic stem cells live up to their promise; however, many people are studying other types of cells and tissues, such as adult stem cells, umbilical cord stem cells, and fetal tissue to cure diseases. The contributors of the viewpoints in this chapter explore the alternatives to embryonic stem cells.

| "If one looks at the human clinical trials or research using experimental animals, the record for adult stem cells compared to embryonic stem cells is extremely impressive."

Adult Stem Cells Are More Promising than Embryonic Stem Cells

Jean Peduzzi-Nelson

In the following viewpoint, Jean Peduzzi-Nelson asserts that adult stem cells have a better record of success than do embryonic stem cells. Peduzzi-Nelson points out the disadvantages of embryonic stem cells and the advantages of adult stem cells. She maintains that although embryonic stem cells get the most attention, adult stem cells have quietly put together an impressive list of results. Jean Peduzzi-Nelson is a professor in the Department of Anatomy and Cell Biology at the Wayne State University School of Medicine in Detroit.

Jean Peduzzi-Nelson, "Adult Stem Cells Are Behind Much of Stem Cell Success So Far," *Milwaukee Journal Sentinel.* September 3, 2006. www.jsonline.com. Reproduced by permission of the author.

As you read, consider the following questions:

1. Why does Peduzzi-Nelson say that the potential of embryonic stem cells to turn into any type of cell has little clinical relevance?

2. Why is the "rapid proliferation" of embryonic stem cells both good and bad, according to the author?

3. According to Peduzzi-Nelson, what is one of the problems with embryonic stem cells?

The great potential moral controversies and political party alignments associated with the stem cell issue makes the subject a hot topic.

Human stem cells can be obtained from human embryos, produced either by in vitro fertilization of human eggs or cloning via somatic cell nuclear transplant, or [from] adults.

Embryonic Stem Cells: So-called Advantages

The often stated advantages of embryonic stem cells are 1) their great promise, 2) their potential to form every cell type, 3) their rapid proliferation, 4) their lack of rejection and finally, 5) their usefulness in drug testing and disease models.

However, from a scientific and medical point of view these advantages are less clear.

The "great promise" of embryonic cells is often stated by scientists that either hold key patents or are strongly supported by biotech companies pursuing embryonic cells commercially.

Every type of stem cell may be useful for injuries but [such cells] are unlikely to cure most diseases, as underlying causes of uncured diseases are often not known. Stem cells may alleviate the symptoms for several years but not affect the disease process. Other areas of research are actively being studied on disease processes so stem cells are not the magic silver bullet in diseases.

The "potential of embryonic stem cells to possibly form every cell type" in the body is amazing but is of little clinical relevance. As long as a stem/progenitor cell is capable of forming the cell types needed for a particular injury or disease, the capability to form every cell type is a moot point.

Furthermore, there are numerous supporting studies [showing] that stem cells derived from adults have the same potential. Sources of adult stem cells include the skin, fat, bone marrow stromal cells, umbilical cord and many other sites in the body.

The "rapid proliferation of embryonic stem cells" is [a] rather ironic claim in that the quality cited for the superiority of embryonic stem cells is actually responsible for causing serious problems. Rapid growth is not always a desirable quality, as clearly seen with weeds in a garden or cancer in the body.

In an animal model of Parkinson's disease, rats injected with embryonic stem cells showed a slight benefit in about 50% of the rats, but one-fifth of the rats died of brain tumors caused by the embryonic stem cells.

The "lack of rejection of embryonic stem cells" is a clever twist of words. It is true that embryonic cells are not rejected. However, to be useful as a therapy, the cell must mature into a particular cell type.

When the cell matures, it is recognized by the immune system as foreign and is rejected. However, it has also been argued that this is the reason for the great need for human cloning (somatic cell nuclear transplant) so the problem of rejection of embryonic stem cell can be avoided.

This field is in its infancy, and only a very few studies have been done to even demonstrate the feasibility of this in experimental animals. Pursuing this extreme measure when the human body is full of stem/progenitor cells that would not be rejected is one of the most absurd directions ever observed in the history of science that is supposedly being promoted to help people.

What Are Adult Stem Cells?

An adult stem cell is an undifferentiated cell found among differentiated cells in a tissue or organ, can renew itself, and can differentiate to yield the major specialized cell types of the tissue or organ. The primary roles of adult stem cells in a living organism are to maintain and repair the tissue in which they are found. Some scientists now use the term somatic stem cell instead of adult stem cell. Unlike embryonic stem cells, which are defined by their origin (the inner cell mass of the blastocyst), the origin of adult stem cells in mature tissues is unknown.

National Institutes of Health, "Stem Cell Basics," 2006.

"Usefulness in drug testing and disease models" is not a reasonable claim because tissue models and drugs need to be tested on mature tissue, not embryonic cells. There are numerous tissue culture model systems of muscle, skin, etc., that are routinely used in drug and disease models.

Adult Stem Cells: Real Advantages

The advantages of stem cells derived from adult stem cells are virtually unknown to the American public. The most profitable, not the best, treatment for people is not surprisingly getting the most publicity.

The greatest advantage of adult stem cells is that it's usually possible to use a person's own stem cells, which is the safest stem cell option for people. This avoids the problems of rejection, disease transmission, chromosomal abnormalities and uncontrolled growth.

One problem with embryonic stem cells that is rarely mentioned is that methods have yet to be developed to grow these cells in a manner that does not induce significant chromosomal abnormalities.

Impressive Results

If one looks at the human clinical trials or research using experimental animals, the record for adult stem cells compared to embryonic stem cells is extremely impressive. In examining only the scientific evidence, one wonders why the controversy even exists.

Parkinson's disease When a transplant consists of embryonic/fetal tissue, the stem/progenitor cells are the only cells that survive. In two clinical trials using embryonic/fetal tissue, devastating deterioration at one year after treatment occurred in about 15% of these patients that was believed to result from cellular overgrowth or from rejection of the foreign cells/tissue derived from embryo or fetus.

These results are in striking contrast to the report on a patient who received his own adult stem cells, who had almost full recovery for several years after the transplant.

In a recent animal study, human embryonic stem cells not only did not cause improvement in an animal model of Parkinson's disease but also caused tumor formation. Another direction of hope for Parkinson's disease is the use of growth factors.

Diabetes Diabetes, like Parkinson's disease, is a disease, so it may not be possible to cure diabetes with any type of stem cells but only dissipate the symptoms for several years. Recently, insulin independence was reported in a person after receiving cells from her mother.

Also encouraging were results found in animal studies [showing] that blocking the autoimmune reaction can reverse diabetes in mice. There are also several reports that adult stem cells can develop into insulin-secreting cells.

Spinal cord injury The comparison of results with adult and embryonic stem cells is even more dramatic. Although mice receiving embryonic stem cells made the front page of many newspapers and extensive web coverage, a paper published by [Mercedes] Zurita and [Jesús] Vaquero found almost total recovery from complete paralysis in rats using adult stem cells from bone marrow. Transplants of tissue containing one's own stem cells is safe and causes some improvement in people with severe, chronic spinal cord injury.

Heart disease Several recent studies of patients with heart attacks report benefit from adult stem cells derived from bone marrow. Clinical trials have also shown improvements in some patients with heart failure after using one's own adult stem cells in treatment.

Quiet Success

Similar comparisons can be made for a variety of diseases and injuries. But the successes with adult stem cells will never make headlines or be heard by the majority of the American public.

Although it may take years for these adult stem cell treatments to be commonly available, the results with adult stem cells will eventually end a controversy that should never have existed in the first place. The controversy may end even sooner than that . . . [if] embryonic stem cells can be derived from sperm, as reported in . . . *Nature*.

"Some people contend that adult stem cells hold more promise than [embryonic] stem cells. This is simply not true."

Adult Stem Cells Are Not More Promising than Embryonic Stem Cells

William B. Neaves

In the following viewpoint, William B. Neaves testifies to the Judiciary Committee of the Missouri State Senate concerning legislation that would prohibit human somatic nuclear transfer (SCNT), a technique used to create embryonic stem cells. Supporters of the bill had previously testified that adult stem cells are more promising than embryonic stem cells derived using the SCNT procedure. Neaves asserts that studying adult stem cells will not reveal the mechanisms underlying the earliest human development, nor can they provide clues as to how nonspecialized cells develop into specialized cells. He argues that there is no debate among scientists: Adult stem cells are worthy of study and can provide many treatments, but they cannot replace embryonic stem cells. William B. Neaves is the president and CEO of the Stowers Institute for Medical Research in Kansas City, Missouri.

William B. Neaves, "Testimony to the Judiciary Committee of the Missouri Senate," www.kcchamber.com, January 31, 2005. Reproduced by permission of the Greater Kansas City Chamber of Commerce and the author.

As you read, consider the following questions:

1. Neaves states that researchers are unable to find adult stem cells in what organ?
2. Which type of stem cell discovered so far has the ability to develop into every specialized cell and tissue in the human body, according to the author?
3. According to Neaves, in what year was the first therapeutic bone marrow transplant performed?

Some people contend that adult stem cells hold more promise than early stem cells. This is simply not true. Stem cells occur in some adult tissues and organs, but the search for these cells has been frustrating in other vital organs, such as the pancreas, where none has yet been found. Where they do exist, their developmental potential is restricted to the cell types typically found in that organ or tissue. In spite of years of intense effort, no one has discovered a population of stem cells in the adult body or in umbilical cord blood that can develop into every specialized cell and tissue in the body. From time to time, preliminary reports hold out the possibility of such a discovery, but attempts to document and reproduce such findings have so far failed.

Only Embryonic Stem Cells Can Provide Clues to Early Development

Only early stem cells from blastocysts [embryos] have the demonstrated potential to become any specialized cell in the body. Leading adult stem cell scientists like Dr. Irving Weissman at Stanford will verify this, as will the Director of the National Institutes of Health, Dr. Elias Zerhouni, who wrote the following in the May 9, 2003 issue of *Science*:

> The U.S. National Institutes of Health place a high priority on support for research using human embryonic stem cells, as well as other types of stem cells, that will also be useful for basic, translational, and clinical studies. Research using

Cures Require Embryonic Stem Cells

Adult stem cells are used to treat some types of disease, including leukemia and other blood diseases. We believe that scientists should study adult stem cells in areas where they show promise. However, most of the nation's top scientists and institutions agree that embryonic stem cells are more likely to treat a wide range of diseases and injuries.

Also, stem cell based treatments will require many cells that are safe, stable and identical. Adult stem cells do not exist in large numbers and so aren't available to treat the millions of people living with disease. To create as many cells as we will need, scientists must direct stem cells to divide many, many times. Adult stem cells cannot divide over time and create stable cells. It is extremely hard to isolate and grow adult cells in the lab. Scientists believe embryonic stem cells are the only realistic supply for practical cell-based therapies.

Alliance for Stem Cell Research, "Stem Cell Facts."
www.curesforcalifornia.com.

human embryonic stem cells offers the potential to inform us about the earliest molecular and cellular processes that regulate normal development and provides a tool to discover how a cell is able to be both pluripotent and indefinitely self-renewing. In addition, research using human embryonic stem cells will help the scientific community to understand the molecular signals that specify differentiation into specific cell types, some of which may ultimately be useful for cell-based treatment of disorders that involve loss of a specific cell type (such as type 1 diabetes or Parkinson's disease, to cite two of many examples).

Adult Stem Cell Research Is Not a Substitute

Opponents frequently try to pit research with adult stem cells against research with early stem cells. I work at an organization that has a huge investment in adult stem cell research. In 2003, the Stowers Institute in Kansas City was the site of the discovery of the long-sought bone marrow stem cell niche, a discovery that the editors of *Nature* credited with resolving a quarter-century-long quest. This discovery, made five decades after adult bone marrow stem cell therapy was first attempted, may help make adult stem cell therapy more effective in cures that require regeneration of the blood cells. Hence, research with adult stem cells holds great interest for medicine, but any of the scientists conducting adult stem cell research at the Stowers Institute will quickly say that it is no substitute for research with early stem cells, the only stem cells yet discovered that can develop into every specialized cell and tissue in the body. . . .

Scientists Are Not Divided about Stem Cells

Those who would pit research with adult stem cells against research with early stem cells are trying to mislead laypeople. The overwhelming majority of scientists and physicians in the U.S. support research with both adult and early stem cells. The organizations to which they belong support research with early stem cells, including those produced by SCNT [somatic cell nuclear transfer]. These include the American Medical Association, the National Medical Association, the Association of American Medical Schools, the Institute of Medicine of the National Academy of Sciences, and the National Academy of Sciences itself. The fact that a handful of scientists may oppose research with early stem cells does not reflect a division of scientific opinion on this issue. Sixty winners of the Nobel Prize, the most distinguished award a scientist can receive, have publicly endorsed SCNT stem cell research. There is no list of Nobel Laureates who oppose SCNT, and there is no real "scientific debate" about the worthiness of research with early stem cells. . . .

The overwhelming majority of scientists and physicians strongly support research with SCNT. They and the patients suffering from degenerative diseases and debilitating injuries believe, as . . . I do, that research with SCNT must continue.

Adult Stem Cells: Still Low Success Rate

Proponents of [Missouri's proposed legislation] say there is no need to seek cures with SCNT stem cells. They say SCNT stem cells have never been used to treat any disease, while adult stem cells have helped patients with a variety of diseases. Research with adult stem cell therapy in the form of bone marrow transplantation has been underway for more than 50 years. Dr. E. Donnall Thomas performed the first therapeutic bone marrow transplant in 1956 and received the Nobel Prize for his pioneering work in 1990. Twenty-five years ago, Dr. Steve Teitelbaum, a distinguished medical scientist from Washington University whom the members of the Senate Judiciary Committee know, participated in the first use of adult bone marrow stem cells to cure a fatal childhood disease. Dr. Teitelbaum will tell you that the success rate for cures using adult stem cells is low due to genetic incompatibility between donor and recipient, a problem that SCNT stem cell therapy avoids. Dr. Teitelbaum is an enthusiastic supporter of research and therapy using SCNT, as are the overwhelming majority of medical scientists and physicians everywhere.

Developing Cures Takes Years of Research

The first report of early stem cells produced by SCNT was published [in 2004]. Developing cures takes years of research. It does not happen overnight. If research with bone marrow transplantation had been outlawed 50 years ago, the proponents of [the proposed legislation] would have no list of adult stem cell cures to show you. One thing we can predict with absolute certainty. If research and treatment with SCNT stem cells is outlawed, they will never save someone's life.

I am reminded of the status of penicillin therapy in 1941. No human being had yet been treated with the new antibiotic. Four years later, the lives of tens of thousands of allied military personnel had been saved by penicillin. Imagine how short-sighted it would have been in 1941 if someone had introduced legislation to criminalize penicillin research on the grounds that the old sulfa drugs had treated a number of infectious diseases, but no one had yet been saved by penicillin.

The leading scientists in the field of adult stem cell research in the U.S. and around the world strongly support research with early stem cells. These include Irving Weissman at Stanford, David Scadden at Harvard, Ihor Lemischka at Princeton, Catherine Verfaillie at Minnesota, Mervin Yoder at Indiana, and Robert Casper at Toronto. Please be aware that proponents of [the proposed legislation] actually list publications from these adult stem cell scientists to support their argument that research with early stem cells is unnecessary. When these scientists learn of this misuse of their name and their work, they object strenuously, as did Dr. Robert Casper in his letter of January 19, 2005, to Missouri Representative Jim Lembke. This letter was in response to Representative Lembke's communication to members of the Missouri General Assembly indicating Dr. Casper did not see the need for research with early stem cells. Dr. Casper is a leading researcher in the field of umbilical cord stem cells, and in that letter, he concludes by saying, "Far from condemning embryonic stem cell research, I support this research and would deplore any attempt to criminalize it."

"Although fetal stem cells are still not fully understood, many scientists believe they might offer advantages that other stem cells don't."

Fetal Stem Cells Are a Promising Alternative to Embryonic Stem Cells

BusinessWeek

In the following viewpoint, BusinessWeek reports that scientific research indicates that fetal stem cells are the most promising type of stem cells. Fetal stem cells contain the malleability of embryonic stem cells and the stability and nontumor-forming character of adult stem cells. According to BusinessWeek, researchers are excited about the possibility that fetal stem cells will be programmed to turn into heart cells and thus cure many types of heart disease. BusinessWeek is a weekly business-oriented newsmagazine.

As you read, consider the following questions:

1. Why does Barnett Suskind perform fetal stem cell research in Barbados instead of the United States, according to *BusinessWeek*?

2. According to the author, what is the age of a fetus that fetal stem cells normally come from?

3. Why are scientists excited about implanting fetal stem cells in the hearts of people waiting for heart transplants, according to *BusinessWeek*?

On June 6, [2005,] a team of scientists release[d] results of a study that they believe could usher in a whole new way of treating heart disease. At a meeting for cardiologists, a surgeon from Lenox Hill Hospital in New York describe[d] what happened when stem cells taken from fetuses were injected into the hearts of 10 patients.

The patients in the study suffer from heart failure, a debilitating and as-yet incurable disease that afflicts 500,000 Americans. The data from the study can't be unveiled quite yet, but Barnett Suskind, CEO of the Institute of Regenerative Medicine in Barbados, believes the results will "compel us to move forward with additional work." Suskind, whose company provided funding for the study, says, "It's absolutely a milestone."

A Friendlier Climate

Many more studies will have to be done before this treatment is anywhere near marketable. Still, Suskind's enthusiasm underscores the growing interest in a controversial but therapeutically promising type of stem cell. So-called fetal-derived stem cells, such as those used in the [above-mentioned] heart study, aren't subject to the same restrictions that limit federal funding for research on embryonic stem cells. But because fetal cells are taken from aborted fetuses, they conjure up much of the emotion that has characterized the current debate [over embryonic stem cells] in Washington. Critics of stem-cell research, in short, oppose any such research that they believe requires the destruction of human life.

Suskind, an American entrepreneur, started his company in Barbados [in 2004] because he feared the political storm

Why Is Fetal Tissue Research Important?

- Due to their capacity to rapidly divide, grow, and adapt to new environments, fetal cells hold unique promise for medical research into a variety of diseases and medical conditions.

- Researchers use fetal tissue to investigate questions of normal fetal development, and also to understand the potential to use fetal tissue to transplant into other humans to treat disease.

- Fetal tissue research has already let to major discoveries in human health and has the potential to continue to benefit mankind.

- Researchers study fetal tissue to learn more about birth defects and diseases. By studying normal and abnormal development in fetal tissue, scientists will learn more about gene activation that may cause mental retardation, Down's Syndrome, SIDS [sudden infant death syndrome], and defective eye development.

- The genes responsible for some diseases of later life, such as Alzheimer's, prostate cancer, and Type II diabetes, may be activated during fetal development.

- There is hope that fetal tissue transplanted into patients with illnesses such as Parkinson's diabetes or heart disease may be a valuable treatment.

American Society for Cell Biology,
"Fetal Tissue Facts." www.ascb.org.

surrounding stem cells in the U.S. would make it difficult to do business in his home country. "The government here [in Barbados] has welcomed us," Suskind says. "We can conduct our work with their blessing." Although fetal cells are technically different from embryonic stem cells, "most people use the terms interchangeably, and that could present problems," he points out.

What makes fetal stem cells different from the embryonic variety is age. The former come from fetuses that are about eight weeks old. That means they're more fully developed than embryonic stem cells. Although fetal stem cells are still not fully understood, many scientists believe they might offer advantages that other stem cells don't. Embryonic cells, for example, are complete blank slates, meaning they hold the potential to turn into any type of tissue. But that flexibility is exactly what makes them difficult to manipulate.

What Is Going On?

On the other end of the spectrum are adult stem cells, which are often taken from bone marrow. These cells are already somewhat programmed, so they can turn into only a more limited variety of tissues.

Fetal stem cells may fall somewhere in between. Early studies suggest they're not quite as flexible as embryonic stem cells, yet they may be somewhat more programmable than adult stem cells. And in heart failure, that quality could be vital. Several studies have been conducted in which adult stem cells have been implanted in patients' damaged hearts. Some patients improve significantly, but others don't, and no one understands why.

Furthermore, researchers aren't quite sure what the adult stem cells turn into once they lodge in the heart. They might be morphing into blood vessels that improve blood flow through damaged tissue. In some studies, the adult stem cells seem to attach to existing heart cells and then strengthen them. But the outstanding questions—and controversy over just how much these cells actually make patients feel better—have left some scientists unconvinced that adult stem cells can really offer a cure for heart disease.

"A Lot to Learn"

Scientists who have worked on studies with Suskind's institute believe fetal cells might go one step further. "Fetal cells are younger [than adult cells], and these young cells are more powerful," says Federico Benetti, who has conducted studies of both adult and fetal stem cells in Argentina, Uruguay, and Ecuador. Benetti believes the fetal cells may be prompting new heart muscle to grow—something no heart therapy has come close to achieving. Still, he's careful to add: "We have a lot to learn. This has opened the window to continue investigating."

Suskind says the next step will be to conduct studies that are "a little more rigorous." He can't estimate how long it will take to prove the therapy works, but he's confident that if the science succeeds, "the treatment will be mainstreamed very quickly."

Scientists elsewhere are also working to gain a better understanding of exactly what stem cells do once they're implanted in damaged hearts. Researchers at the University of Pittsburgh's McGowen Institute for Regenerative Medicine are especially excited about an upcoming study in which they'll implant adult stem cells in patients waiting for heart transplants. Once these patients receive their transplants, their old hearts will go to McGowen's scientists, who'll slice into the hearts, track down the implanted stem cells, literally, and study them to try to determine how they help repair damaged hearts.

"The only way to know for sure is to start taking hearts out," says McGowen's Dr. Amit Patel. It will be one small but important step in the continuing quest to put stem cells to work in healing hearts—and to determine exactly which type of cells will prove most useful.

| *"Most Americans . . . are not ready to approve the macabre practice of 'fetus farming' [for stem cells]."*

Stem Cells Should Not Be Harvested from Artificially Grown Fetuses

Robert P. George

In the following viewpoint, Robert P. George argues that the United States must ban "fetus farming"—the practice of harvesting stem cells from aborted fetuses—immediately. Otherwise, he contends, fetal tissue transplants may begin to save lives and cure diseases, and Americans might become numb to the gruesome practice. George believes that the threat of fetus farming is real and imminent because stem cells from early (five-day-old) embryos have problems that prevent them from being used in therapies; problems not found with fetal stem cells. Robert P. George is a professor of jurisprudence and the director of the James Madison Program in American Ideals and Institutions at Princeton University.

As you read, consider the following questions:

1. Why does George say that biomedical scientists are interested in fetus farming?
2. Why does the author say that early embryonic stem cells cannot be used for therapeutic purposes?
3. What does George say is the best legislation to prevent fetus farming?

The journal *Science* [in September 2005] published the results of research conducted at Harvard proving that embryonic stem cells can be produced by a method that does not involve creating or destroying a living human embryo. Additional progress will be required to perfect this technique of stem cell production, but few seriously doubt that it will be perfected, and many agree that this can be accomplished in the relatively near future. At the same time, important breakthroughs have been announced by scientists at the University of Pittsburgh and the University of Texas demonstrating that cells derived harmlessly from placental tissue and umbilical cord blood can be induced to exhibit the pluripotency of embryonic stem cells. ("Pluripotency" is the potential of a cell to develop into multiple types of mature cells.)

One would expect that advocates of embryonic stem cell research would be delighted by these developments. After all, they point to uncontroversial ways to obtain embryonic stem cells or their exact equivalent and to create new stem cell lines that are (unlike lines created by destroying embryos) immediately eligible for federal funding. Yet some advocates seem to be unhappy at the news. Why?

The likely answer is ominous.

Fetus Farming Is the Real Goal

Up to now, embryonic stem cell advocates have claimed that they are only interested in stem cells harvested from embryos at the blastocyst (or five-to six-day) stage. They have denied any intention of implanting embryos either in the uterus of a volunteer or in an artificial womb in order to harvest cells, tissues, or organs at more advanced stages of embryonic development or in the fetal stage. Advocates are well aware that "most Americans, including those who are prepared to countenance the destruction of very early embryos, are not ready to approve the macabre practice of 'fetus farming.'" However, based on the literature I have read and the evasive answers given by spokesmen for the biotechnology industry at meetings of the President's Council on Bioethics, I fear that the long-term goal is indeed to create an industry in harvesting late embryonic and fetal body parts for use in regenerative medicine and organ transplantation.

This would explain why some advocates of embryonic stem cell research are not cheering the news about alternative sources of pluripotent stem cells. If their real goal is fetus farming, then the cells produced by alternative methods will not serve their purposes.

Why Fetus Farming?

Why would biomedical scientists be interested in fetus farming? Researchers know that stem cells derived from blastocyst-stage embryos are currently of no therapeutic value and may never actually be used in the treatment of diseases. (In a candid admission, South Korean cloning expert Curie Ahn recently said that developing therapies may take "three to five decades.")

In fact, there is not a single embryonic stem cell therapy even in clinical trials. (By contrast, adult and umbilical cord stem cells are already being used in the treatment of 65 diseases.) All informed commentators know that embryonic stem cells cannot be used in therapies because of their tendency to generate dangerous tumors. However, recent studies show that the problem of tumor formation does not exist in cells taken from cows, mice, and other mammals when embryos have been implanted and extracted after several weeks or months of development (i.e. have been gestated to the late embryonic or fetal stage). This means that the real therapeutic potential lies precisely in the practice of fetus farming. Because the developmental process stabilizes cells (which is why we are not all masses of tumors), it is likely true that stem cells, tissues, and organs harvested from human beings at, say, 16 or 18 weeks or later *could* be used in the treatment of diseases.

Scientists associated with a leading firm in the embryonic stem cell field, Advanced Cell Technology, recently published a research paper discussing the use of stem cells derived from cattle fetuses that had been produced by cloning (to create a genetic match). Although the article did not mention human beings, it was plain that the purpose of the research was not to cure diseased cows, but rather to establish the potential therapeutic value of doing precisely the same thing with human beings. For those who have ears to hear, the message is clear. I am hardly the first to perceive this message. *Slate* magazine bioethics writer Will Saletan drew precisely the same conclusion in a remarkable five-part series, the final installment of which was entitled "The Organ Factory: The Case for Harvesting Older Human Embryos."

We Must Ban It

If we do not put into place a legislative ban on fetus farming, public opposition to the practice could erode. People *now* find it revolting. But what will happen to public sentiment if the research is permitted to go forward and in fact generates treatments for some dreadful diseases or afflictions? I suspect that those in the biotech industry who do look forward to fetus farming are betting that moral opposition will collapse when the realistic prospect of cures is placed before the public.

Scientists Nearing Headless-Clone Farms

In 1997 an article in the *New York Times* stated that headless human cloning for organ harvesting would occur within ten years. Scientists now claim to be close to that goal. Speaking at the Conquest Over Mortality conference of the International College of Surgeons, P.B. Desai, an oncologist and former director of the Mumbai-based Tata Memorial Centre said it is just a matter of time until human organ farms are available for researchers and doctors. He pointed to research done in mice in which the genes that control development of the head are removed. Desai said, "the body would [still] have the capacity to keep the organs functional for use as transplants." Desai claimed that "The ultimate aim of science and medicine is towards immortality" and said that headless clones were preferable to embryonic stem cell treatments: "Embryonic stem cells, which holds promise of cure of any organ, is but a slow move towards immortality."

The Interim, *"Science Nearing Headless Clonal Farms,"* December 2004. www.theinterim.com. Reproduced by permission.

The ideal legislation to protect human life and preserve public moral sensibilities would ban all production of human embryos for research in which they are destroyed. Unfortunately, Congress is not prepared to pass such legislation. Indeed, a bill passed by the House of Representatives to ban the production of human embryos, for any purpose, by cloning has been stymied in the Senate. (In this one instance, many American liberals decline to follow the lead of Europe—where many jurisdictions ban all human cloning, including the creation of embryos by cloning for biomedical research—or of the United Nations General Assembly, which has called for a complete cloning ban.) So what can be done?

One possibility is to make a pre-emptive strike against fetus farming by banning the initiation of any pregnancy (whether in a human uterus or artificial womb) for purposes other than the live birth of a child. This has been recommended by the President's Council on Bioethics. Another possible approach would be to add to the safeguards already in the U.S. Code on fetal tissue, stating that it is unlawful for anyone to use, or engage in interstate commerce in, such tissue when the person knows that the pregnancy was initiated in order to produce this tissue. An effective strategy would eliminate what would otherwise almost certainly emerge as a powerful incentive for the production of thousands of embryos that would be destroyed in perfecting and practicing cloning and fetal farming.

A Critical Juncture

My suspicions and sense of urgency have been heightened by the fact that my home state of New Jersey has passed a bill that specifically authorizes and encourages human cloning for, among other purposes, the harvesting of "cadaveric fetal tissue." A "cadaver," of course, is a dead body. The bodies in question are those of fetuses created by cloning specifically to be gestated and killed as sources of tissues and organs. What the bill envisages and promotes, in other words, is fetus farming. The biotechnology industry put an enormous amount of money into pushing this bill through the New Jersey legislature and is now funding support for similar bills in states around the country.

So we find ourselves at a critical juncture. On the one hand, techniques for obtaining pluripotent stem cells without destroying embryos will, it appears, soon eliminate any plausible argument for killing pre-implantation embryos. This is great news. On the other hand, these developments have, if I am correct, smoked out the true objectives of at least some who have been leading the charge for embryonic stem cell research. Things cannot remain as they are. The battle over embryonic stem cell research will determine whether we as a people move in the direction of restoring our sanctity of life ethic, or go in precisely the opposite direction. Either we will protect embryonic human life more fully than we do now, or we will begin creating human beings precisely as "organ factories." Those of us on the pro-life side must take the measure of the problem quickly so that we can develop and begin implementing a strategy that takes the nation in the honorable direction.

| "Cord blood offers superior benefits over embryonic stem cells."

Umbilical Cord Stem Cells Are More Beneficial than Embryonic Stem Cells

Peter Hollands, interviewed by Peter J. Smith

In the following viewpoint, Peter J. Smith, a reporter for Lifesite-News.com, an alternative online news source, reports on his interview with Peter Hollands, the chief science officer for the United Kingdom Cord Blood Bank. Hollands believes that umbilical cord blood, preserved immediately after the birth of a baby, offers the greatest hope for stem cell therapies; however, he notes, only a small fraction of umbilical cords are actually saved; most are discarded as medical waste. Hollands asserts that the public needs to be made aware of the superior benefits of cord blood stem cells, especially when compared with embryonic stem cells.

As you read, consider the following questions:

1. According to Hollands, cord blood stem cells are capable of repairing what kinds of tissues?

Peter Hollands, interviewed by Peter J. Smith, "UK Researcher: Embryonic Stem Cells Have Never Been Used to Treat Anyone and No Plans Exist to Do So," *LifeSiteNews.com*, August 18, 2006. Reproduced by permission.

2. Why does Hollands take issue with the statement that patient therapies will come from embryonic stem cells?

3. What does Hollands say is the cause of confusion over stem cells?

In an exclusive interview with LifeSiteNews.com, Dr. Peter Hollands, Chief Science Officer of the UK Cord Blood Bank and an early pioneer of (non-human) embryonic stem cell research, spoke about the great strides being made for patients suffering from cancer and disease through stem cell therapies using the morally acceptable cord blood.

Cord Blood Transplants

"Cord blood stem cells have currently been transplanted just over 6000 times worldwide in the treatment of 45 different diseases," stated Dr. Hollands. "These diseases are currently blood disorders and also the repair of the bone marrow following high dose chemotherapy for cancer."

"The most dramatic cord blood transplant is perhaps that of Patrizia Durante who developed leukemia during pregnancy and was transplanted with her own babies' cord blood stem cells," said Dr. Hollands. . . .

Stem cells from cord blood come from blood in the placenta and umbilical cord. Once the cord is cut and both mother and child are well taken care of, a simple procedure collects the cord blood into a special collection bag, which is then processed, frozen and stored in a special laboratory. However, Dr. Hollands laments that cord blood is discarded too often as biological waste in approximately 98% of deliveries.

"This is a massive waste of life-saving stem cells on a daily basis which we must all work to resolve."

Dr. Hollands revealed that researchers at the Laurentian University in Ontario are preparing the next breakthrough in stem cell research through a clinical trial testing the ability of

Cord Blood Research: No Conspiracy

Some patient advocates I have spoken with concerning the actions of the NIH [National Institutes of Health] and FDA [Food and Drug Administration] think there is something sinister afoot, indicative of corruption or even conspiracy to keep cord blood stem cell research on the proverbial back burner. In this writer's opinion, the events and actions that have played out against cord blood and cord blood stem cells do not reflect a conspiracy but, rather, a way of doing business; a mechanism that works but which can lead to blind spots, tunnel vision and bottlenecks.

Anthony G. Payne, quoted in World *magazine, February 8, 2005.*

cord blood stem cells to treat Multiple Sclerosis (MS), a debilitating disease which affects 400,000 Americans and 2.5 million persons worldwide.

"If successful, this trial will revolutionize cord blood stem cell technology worldwide," said Dr. Hollands, who is Scientific Advisor to the project supported by Cells for Life.

Flexible and Adaptable

According to Dr. Hollands, the secret of cord blood's success lies with very adaptable cells found in cord blood called "mesenchymal stem cells." These stem cells—found also in the umbilical cord itself—have an immature quality, which makes them very flexible and adaptable in transplants, and can have at least a 50% donor-mismatch.

"These stem cells can produce a whole range of tissue types making cord blood stem cells capable of repairing such things as nerve tissue, muscle (skeletal and cardiac), connective tissue and endocrine cells such as insulin secreting cells. This means that in cord blood we have . . . just as much potential as embryonic stem cells but without all of the related objections and technical concerns." Dr. Hollands indicated that the process has an 80% success rate and not one of the 6000 cord blood recipients have ever developed transplant-related tumors, a lethal reality in embryonic stem cell therapies. . . .

"As a scientist, and even as a lay person, it is simple to see that cord blood as a source of stem cells for therapy and research is the easiest route to take," says Dr. Hollands. "We have a never ending supply of cord blood and if we can start to collect and store this valuable resource instead of discarding it then we will start to make real progress in stem cell therapy and research."

Embryonic Stem Cell Nonsense

However, Dr. Hollands takes issue with those who contend that patient therapies can be obtained from human embryonic stem cells.

"To claim that there are enough 'spare' embryos in IVF [in vitro fertilization] clinics is nonsense," says Dr. Hollands. "These embryos could not support the demand for stem cell transplants," adding [that] embryonic stem cells also have a tendency "to form tumors on transplantation."

He adds, "It is important to note that embryonic stem cells have never been used to treat anyone and that there are no plans to do so. In the UK for example we have invested millions in a national stem cell bank which contains approximately 6 different embryonic stem cell lines, none of which are suitable for transplant."

Dr. Hollands says that embryonic stem cell researchers have taken advantage of the public ignorance about stem cells.

"Currently the average person thinks that embryonic stem cells are the only option available . . . [believing] if we are going to help those people suffering from disease then we have no option but to pursue embryonic stem cell technology. This is completely incorrect," maintains Dr. Hollands.

He adds, "If the public knew that there is a source of stem cells, available at the birth of every child in the world, which carry no risk at all to anyone in their collection or production, then there would be immense public pressure to support cord blood stem cell technology."

Education about Cord Blood Needed

Believing that the media and celebrities are responsible for the current confusion about stem cells, Dr. Hollands advocates a counter strategy using the media and celebrities to educate and inform the public about the superior benefits of cord blood as a source of stem cells. Dr. Hollands says a five-pronged strategy would include:

- prime time TV/radio reports/interviews

- public education campaigns (TV/radio/media/posters/ Internet)

- celebrity endorsement of cord blood stem cell technology (a key ally for embryonic stem cell researchers)

- politicians campaigning for cord blood stem technology

- Newspaper reports on cord blood stem cell technology

Dr. Hollands argues that once the people are made aware that cord blood offers superior benefits over embryonic stem cells then "embryonic stem cell groups will find it impossible to justify their actions."

However, he believes that a real turnaround in the stem cell debate "needs someone, at the highest level, to realize that the wrong path has been chosen and to have the courage to change."

"Rightly or wrongly there has been a massive investment in embryonic stem cell technology in time, money and resources," says Dr. Hollands, adding that many scientists have built their careers around human embryonic stem cell research.

"We should be focusing our time, money and expertise on cord blood stem cell technology," says Dr. Hollands. "The sooner we stop wasting precious resources on embryonic stem cell research the sooner we will have stem cell cures for the people who really matter in all of this—the patients."

| "The possibility of using one's own cord blood stem cells for regenerative medicine is currently purely hypothetical."

Umbilical Cord Stem Cells Cannot Replace Embryonic Stem Cells

K. Welte, World Marrow Donor Association

The World Marrow Donor Association (WMDA) argues in the following viewpoint that many private commercial umbilical cord blood banks are using misleading advertising about potential therapeutic stem cell therapies to get expectant mothers to bank their baby's cord blood. The WMDA contends that the stem cells found in cord blood, called hematopoietic stem cells, are not pluripotent, meaning they are not capable of becoming a variety of other types of cell. Cord blood stem cells, maintains the WMDA, are unlikely to be used in the type of regenerative medicine being touted for embryonic stem cells. The WMDA is an international organization of cord blood banks, registries, and other organizations interested in hematopoietic (blood cell–making) stem cell transplantation.

K. Welte, World Marrow Donor Association, "WMDA Policy Statement for the Utility of Autologous or Family Cord Blood Unit Storage: Explanatory Report of the Cord Blood Registries Subcommittee," May 2006. www.worldmarrow.org. Reproduced by permission.

As you read, consider the following questions:

1. What are the three different types of cord blood banking, according to the WMDA?
2. How much does private cord blood banking generally cost, in the author's reckoning?
3. What is one marketing claim made by private cord blood banks that the WMDA takes issue with?

Many WMDA member organizations facilitate transplants of umbilical cord blood units (CBUs) as well as adult donor marrow and peripheral blood stem cells (PBSC) in their own country and internationally. Approximately 70% of patients with blood disorders such as leukemia, severe aplastic anemia and congenital or other acquired disorders will not have a suitable family donor. These patients rely on public donor registries around the world to provide the adult or umbilical cord hematopoietic cells needed to restore their immune system after receiving the chemotherapy and/or radiation treatment that may cure their disease. The worldwide exchange of adult donor cells and CBUs for transplantation has functioned efficiently and relies on the altruistic donation of these cells from donors who do not know who their recipient is.

There are three different types of cord blood storage:

1. Public cord blood banking
2. Medically indicated, directed family cord blood storage
3. Autologous or family storage (private cord blood banking)

Public Cord Blood Banking

Cord blood unit donation and storage for public unrelated, *allogeneic (cells coming from a person other than the patient)* use is a newer and growing donation option. Today, there are a number of countries that offer public programs for collection and storage of these cells by cord blood banks. These banks store cells for use by patients who need a transplant from an unrelated donor. Many registry members of the WMDA list these CBUs and make them available for their domestic patients and other patients throughout the world. More than 1,500 transplants occur annually worldwide with unrelated CBUs. This number is growing each year.

Public CBU storage is supported by many professional organisations and national governments, and there is extensive medical and scientific documentation of usage of unrelated CBUs for transplantation. Some governments also provide funding to support public CBU storage.

Medically Indicated, Directed Family Cord Blood Storage

A number of cord blood banks offer CBU storage to families who are expecting another baby and already have a sibling with a disease that is potentially treatable with an allogeneic cord blood transplant. The rationale is that if the new baby's HLA [human leukocyte antigen] type is compatible with the affected sibling, cord blood has the potential to be a good source of cells for transplant for the donor's sibling. The likelihood that a sibling will share both HLA haplotypes [sets of closely related genes] is 25%.

When there is a clear medical indication for the storage of directed CBUs there is a significant probability of using those stored units. This is especially likely in siblings that are affected by malignant, genetic or immune disorders. The Children's Hospital Oakland Research Institute, Sibling Donor Program carefully screens families before storing a unit for potential family use. In late 2004, it reported having shipped 41 of 1,266 (1:31) units that were used for transplantation. Other hospitals may have higher use rates, particularly if the original indication for transplantation is clear.

Some transplant centers don't strongly recommend this donation option because the hematopoietic stem cells could be collected from the sibling at a later time if they were actually needed. However, storage of cord blood from a sibling of an affected child may provide a valuable source of cells with quite a high likelihood of use. They are also collected at no risk to the infant donor.

Autologous or Family Storage (Private Cord Blood Banking)

Private cord blood storage companies have developed in many countries to sell cord blood storage to families for potential future *autologous (patient's own cells)* or family use. This is called "private storage" because the units are collected and stored solely to be available for the individual donor or the immediate family. These companies charge a collection fee, generally between $1000–$1500 USD and an annual storage fee, often approximately $100. Some companies also provide financial incentives to health care professionals who recruit their potential customers and bonuses based on the number of successfully collected units.

Companies advertise and promote their programs to pregnant women. Some companies have used sales approaches that appear focused on making the family feel that they are not being good parents if they don't store their baby's cord blood for future use. . . .

Unlikely to Use Autologous Cord Blood

Several governing bodies, notably the European Union and individual members of the Union and some professional organizations, such as the American Academy of Pediatrics and the American College of Obstetricians and Gynecologists have adopted policy statements about the ethics and utility of private and public storage of umbilical cord blood. The general conclusion is that because of the very low probability of autologous use for diseases treatable by transplantation today, and for lack of medical and scientific documentation of autologous cord blood usage, storing cord blood is not recommended and families should not feel pressured to store autologous cord blood. . . .

Cord Blood Stem Cell Therapies Unlikely

Today, no one really knows how cord blood cells might in all aspects be useful in the future and how they will compare to future use of other cell types that are also being used in research today. Private cord blood banks claim that these cells may be used for many diseases in the future. Some private banks indicate these cells can be stored for any member of the family, downplaying the role HLA matching plays in cells used for transplantation.

Many private cord blood banks advertise that autologous cord blood stem cells might be used in the (near) future in reparative or replacement stem cell therapy protocols for various kinds of severe diseases. Although the field of basic stem cell research is rapidly moving forward, there is at present no known protocol where autologous cord blood stem cells are used in therapy. Indeed, the future role of autologous stem cells in new treatment protocols is still very unclear.

Further, if autologous stem cell therapies should become reality in the future, these protocols will probably rely on generally and easily accessible stem cells, and requirements for standards concerning collection, manipulation, storage, quality assessment etc. would be defined in detail to comply with criteria for good manufacturing practice (GMP). It would therefore probably be difficult to accept cord blood cells cryopreserved several years ago under conditions not in compliance with GMP standards and a given protocol. Thus, stem cell therapy protocols should be developed before cell sources are defined and collection methods developed for these treatment modules.

Marketing Makes You Feel Guilty

When Marla Dalton was expecting, she read the pregnancy magazines, picked up pamphlets at her doctor's office and logged on to mom-centric Web sites and chat rooms. In the process, she was inundated by marketing imploring her to privately store her twins' umbilical cord blood.

Was this really a once-in-a-lifetime opportunity to capture blood rich with stem cells that could potentially save the twins or a family member from serious diseases and conditions, she wondered. Was it worth the collection and processing fees, many ranging from $1,000 to $1,740 per child? Plus a likely $95 annual storage fee.

"It was really stressful. The marketing makes you feel guilty," the 41-year old engineer said. "There is this feeling that if you don't do it, you are not doing something to save your child's life."

The marketing works. The private blood banking industry is expanding although many medical experts criticize the companies for exploiting parents' paranoia. Many doctors advise healthy families not to succumb to promotions because the likelihood of ever using the blood is rare, future medical uses for it are uncertain and storage standards can be lacking.

Associated Press, CBSNews.com, April 13, 2004. www.cbsnews.com.

Exaggerated Claims

One of the major issues raised in many of the existing policy statements regarding autologous cord blood storage is that of false or misleading advertisement. Advertising materials often fail to differentiate between unrelated and autologous hematopoietic stem cell (HSC) transplantation, and there is a strong tendency to over-interpret data from basic stem cell research.

Advertisements imply that the indications for unrelated transplantation also hold true for autologous transplants as well, which is not the case.

Many marketing materials make exaggerated claims about how likely the units are to be used in the future. They use advances in embryonic stem cell (ESC) research as an argument to promote autologous cord blood storage. The progress made in ESC research is very promising and may hold the key to the future treatment of many serious diseases. Yet, what advertising materials fail to clarify is that ESCs are *pluripotent (capable of becoming any type of cell)* stem cells derived from early embryos and data from ESC research cannot be transferred to HSC or other stem cell populations found in the CBU. Stem cells from embryos are not used for marrow or peripheral blood or umbilical cord blood transplants.

Furthermore, many companies fail to clarify that HSC or other stem cell populations used in many studies, such as those where stem cells are tested for treatment of adult diseases such as cardiovascular disorders, are collected from the patient's own bone marrow. It is thus very important that families and individuals receive accurate information that distinguishes between the potential for use of currently accepted medical therapies using CBUs and possible future uses, which have not yet been proven or tested in humans.

The European Union (EU) Group in its opinion paper published 16 March, 2004 and titled "Ethical Aspects of Umbilical Cord Blood Banking" based the following statements on such considerations.

1. "Research is taking place into differentiation of pluripotent stem cells into specific cell types which could be used for the treatment of chronic diseases such as Parkinson's, diabetes, cancer, or cardiac infarcts by means of human stem cells but no clear proof of utility of stem cells has been shown." The opinion also states that, "The possibility of using one's own cord blood

stem cells for regenerative medicine is currently purely hypothetical. Research in this field is only at a very early stage." The conclusion of the section on current research is, "It is therefore highly hypothetical that cord blood cells kept for autologous use will be of any value in the future."

2. A portion of the opinion that discusses the ethical aspects of cord blood banking states that, "The legitimacy of commercial cord blood banks for autologous use should be questioned as they sell a service which has presently no real use regarding therapeutic options. Thus they promise more than they can deliver."

"Stem cells that are readily available, perhaps ethically trouble-free and possibly as powerful and flexible in function as their embryonic counterparts [are] 'amniotic-fluid stem cells.'"

Amniotic Fluid Stem Cells May Replace Embryonic Stem Cells

Mary Carmichael

In the following viewpoint, Mary Carmichael reports on a new category of stem cell that some scientists suggest could shake up the field of stem cell research and topple the preeminence of embryonic stem cells. While umbilical cord stem cells and adult stem cells have been offered as alternatives, many people believe that embryonic stem cells hold the most promise for future medical breakthroughs. Carmichael reports, however, that compelling research suggests that fetal stem cells found in the amniotic fluid cushioning the developing human fetus may offer the best hope for curing diseases. Amniotic fluid stem cells appear to be as adaptable and robust as embryonic stem cells, but without the latters' propensity to produce tumors. Furthermore, amniotic *fluid stem cells do not come with the ethical or moral objections associated with embryonic stem cells. Mary Carmichael is a writer for* Newsweek, *a weekly newsmagazine.*

As you read, consider the following questions:

1. According to Carmichael, what does amniocentesis test for, and how many women undergo the procedure?
2. In addition to amniotic fluid, where else are these stem cells found, according to the author?
3. What does Carmichael say are two characteristics that amniotic stem cells have in common with embryonic stem cells?

Stem-cell research is divided into two major camps: one focused on cells from adults, the other on the controversial technique that destroys embryos. But important research published Sunday [January 7, 2007,] supports the idea of a third way, a new category of stem cells that are readily available, perhaps ethically trouble-free and possibly as powerful and flexible in function as their embryonic counterparts: "amniotic-fluid stem cells [AFS]," found in both the placenta and the liquid that surrounds growing fetuses.

The cells are "neither embryonic nor adult. They're somewhere in between," says Dr. Anthony Atala, a tissue-engineering specialist at Wake Forest University who led the research team. (The study appears in the journal *Nature Biotechnology.*) The "AFS cells" rival embryonic stem cells in their ability to multiply and transform into many different cell types, and they eventually could be hugely helpful to doctors in treating diseases throughout the body and building new organs in the lab. At the same time, the amniotic cells can be taken easily and harmlessly from the placenta or from pregnant women by amniocentesis—which gives them the potential to nullify, or at least bridge, the divide in the stem-cell-research debate. One out of every 50 pregnant women undergoes amniocentesis, a procedure that tests the fetus for genetic defects, and about 1 percent of the cells collected by amniocentesis are stem cells. What's more, the stem cells are also found in the placenta, which is thrown away after birth—so doctors may obtain them from all infants, not just those subject to amniocentesis.

All of that means the cells come with little "ethical baggage," says David Prentice, a senior fellow in life sciences at the Family Research Council, which has a long-standing position against embryonic-stem-cell research. "I'm just pumped up by this," adds Prentice. "It's fantastic."

The AFS cells thrive and divide in the amniotic fluid and placenta throughout the gestation process. Scientists have studied them for several years, but the new research is the first to fully characterize them and demonstrate their potential. "What Dr. Atala has done is to present eloquently, for the first time, the real power that these cells have," says Dr. Roger De Filippo, a urologist and tissue engineer at Childrens Hospital Los Angeles who called the research a "sentinel paper."

Similarities with Embryonic Stem Cells

Like those from embryos, the AFS cells are pluripotent, or able to transform into fully-grown cells representing each of the three major kinds of tissue found in the body. Using stem cells taken by amniocentesis from 19 pregnant women, Atala and his colleagues were able to create in the lab nerve cells, liver cells, endothelial cells (which line blood vessels) and cells involved in the creation of bone, muscle and fat. (De Filippo's lab has also coaxed amniotic cells into becoming structures found in the kidneys.) Some of the cells in Atala's lab even functioned as they would be expected to in the human body. The liver cells secreted urea, an activity otherwise seen exclusively in their natural counterparts. And, in a development that may hearten patients with Parkinson's disease and other neurological disorders, the lab's nerve cells secreted glutamate—a neurotransmitter that is crucial to memory and helps to form dopamine, which Parkinson's patients lack. The lab also conducted tests on mice with a neurodegenerative disease and showed that the amniotic cells sought out and re-populated damaged areas of the brain.

Amniotic-fluid stem cells share another unique characteristic with embryonic stem cells: they multiply quickly and are remarkably long-lived. The Atala lab's cells divided more than 250 times—more than quintuple the life expectancy for stem cells taken from adults. Dr. Dario Fauza, a surgeon at Children's Hospital Boston, says he had achieved comparable results working with stem cells from amniotic fluid: "I practically haven't been able to get them to stop growing." The cells are hardy, a trait that makes them relatively easy to culture. "If you think about where they are in nature, they're floating in the amniotic fluid, in which there is very little oxygen," says Fauza. "So they are very tolerant to low oxygen levels, which makes it easier to manipulate them in the lab."

That resilience may eventually help doctors trying to grow new organs or graft tissue into patients. "When you implant an engineered graft, it's typically vulnerable early on, because it takes a few days for the host to send blood vessels to feed it," says Fauza. "So you need a cell that can take that punishment for a while." You also need, says De Filippo, "a lot of cells to create organs"—a demand that the amniotic cells may meet even more easily than embryonic cells can. In addition, for reasons that are still poorly understood, the amniotic cells do not seem to form the tumors known as teratomas that sometimes arise from embryonic stem cells implanted in animals.

Legislative and Ethical Impact

In the short term, Prentice says, the new discovery might not have much legislative impact. "I don't think we're going to see much difference in the rhetoric that both sides will be putting

out," he says. . . . But, he adds, "people are becoming more aware that there is another way to get to what we're all after: helping patients, without the ethical concerns and without the bickering." De Filippo also says the new discoveries would be a boon to "the momentum of stem-cell research, especially in California."

Further down the road, the cells could be ideal candidates for "banking," as an increasing number of new parents do today with blood taken from their babies' umbilical cords. Like cord blood cells, the amniotic cells can be frozen. But once thawed, they live much longer. "The maximum you can do with cord blood cells, which are often used to treat leukemia, is get them to double once," says Atala, compared with the stem cells' lifespan of 250 doublings. A future amniotic stem-cell reserve might be stocked with a variety of genetic types so that cells could be matched to patients with the fewest potential complications.

Cautious Optimism

That era, of course, is well in the future. Many scientists are quick to emphasize that comprehensive human trials are still many years away. It took seven years, Atala notes, just to show the cells' promise, and he declined to estimate how many more it would be before clinical trials could begin, saying, "all those predictions never turn out." There are still many mysteries surrounding amniotic-fluid stem cells—why they don't cause tumors, why they apparently provoke very little immune response when implanted and when during embryonic development they first arise—that might give the FDA [Food and Drug Administration] pause.

Still, a few experiments on human tissue using cells taken from amniotic fluid are currently in the works. Late [in 2006], a Swiss team reported that it had temporarily been able to grow human heart valves from cells found in amniotic fluid. Dr. Fauza has published a number of large animal studies on tissue engineered from AFS cells over the last several years and is now preparing a clinical trial, this one focusing on children born with a hole in their diaphragms. Babies with the defect today have it patched up with Teflon, "which obviously doesn't grow, so the defect often recurs as the child gets older," says Fauza. Instead, he proposes to construct grafts using amniotic stem cells, and then implant them into newborns. He already has seven years worth of data, all of it encouraging, from performing the same operation on sheep. "The FDA is being helpful, but they are also being very cautious," he says. Still, he hopes the trial will begin in "the not-too-distant future." It's a future that's suddenly looking brighter.

Periodical Bibliography

The following articles have been selected to supplement the diverse views presented in this chapter.

Associated Press — "Adult Stem Cells Little or No Help to Heart Repair: Results of Studies Point to Need for Embryonic Stem Cells, Scientists Say," *MSNBC*, 2006. www.msnbc.com.

Ronald Bailey — "A Stem Cell Christmas Miracle? Not Bloody Likely, Alas," *Reason*, December 1, 2004.

Ed Bradley and Hans Keirstead — "Scientist Hopes for Stem Cell Success," *CBS News*, February 26, 2006. www.cbsnews.com.

Janine DeFao — "Is It Worth Banking Your Baby's Cord Blood?" *SFGate.com*, June 20, 2005. www.sfgate.com.

D.M. Deshpande et al. — "Stem Cell Mix Helps Paralyzed Rats Walk," *Technology Review*, September/October 2006.

James P. Kelly — "Stem Cell Politics: Divide and Conquer," *Human Events Online*, September 5, 2006. www.humanevents.com.

Jeanne F. Loring and Catherine Campbell — "Intellectual Property and Human Embryonic Stem Cell Research," *Science*, March 24, 2006.

Don Reed — "Of Lies, Lawyer Lies, and the Adult Stem Cell 'Cure' List," Missouri Coalition for Lifesaving Cures, January 5, 2006. www.missouricures .com.

Wesley J. Smith — "The Great Stem Cell Cover-Up," *Weekly Standard*, August 7, 2006.

Jill Stanek — "Fetus Farming Shot to Hell—Where It Belongs," *WorldNetDaily*, July 26, 2006. www.worldnetdaily.com.

Christian Toto — "Brain Injuries to Newborns," *Washington Times*, August 22, 2006.

For Further Discussion

Chapter 1

1. How do the credentials of an author affect the credibility of her or his viewpoint? For instance, Robert Goldstein is the only author in this chapter that is a physician. Does this influence your impression of his viewpoint? Why or why not?

2. How do the challenges noted by the Stem Cell Research Foundation as needing to be addressed before stem cell research can provide cures compare with the challenges and research setbacks that Peter Aldhous writes about in his viewpoint? Why might the Stem Cell Research Foundation highlight the hopes of stem cell research over the challenges it faces?

3. Robert Goldstein begins his viewpoint by referring to the challenges and fears facing the parents of Jamie Langbein, a young diabetes sufferer. How do you think this affected Goldstein's audience? Do you think using a personal story to begin an argument is effective? Why or why not?

Chapter 2

1. The viewpoints written by Jonathan D. Moreno and Sam Berger and William P. Cheshire explore the morality of sacrificing embryos for stem cell research but come to different conclusions about what is morally acceptable. Which viewpoint do you think is more logical? Which one is more emotional? Which is more persuasive? Why?

2. In their viewpoints, William P. Cheshire and David A. Prentice and William Saunders provide various reasons that have led them to conclude that embryo research and therapeutic cloning are immoral. List the common reasons

used in the two viewpoints and then list any reasons that are unique to one viewpoint or the other. Similarly, list the commonalities and differences between Jonathan D. Moreno and Sam Berger's argument and that of Michael Sandel.

3. Paul Lauritzen argues that stem cell research represents a threat to human rights because it may lead to a society where the human body is seen merely as "material to be manipulated." What do you think Lauritzen was trying to achieve with his essay? Do you think he is arguing against stem cell research? Explain.

4. In his viewpoint, E. Christian Brugger says the ANT-OAR procedure is a moral way to obtain stem cells. Do you think William Cheshire would agree that ANT-OAR is a moral way to obtain embryonic stem cells? Explain your answer.

Chapter 3

1. What basis does George W. Bush use to support his assertion that his policy on embryonic stem cell research is morally sound? Compare Bush's rationale with Arthur Caplan's grounds for saying Bush's policy is morally inconsistent. Which line of reasoning do you think is stronger and why?

2. The number of federally approved stem cell lines is inadequate for research, claims the Juvenile Diabetes Research Foundation. Eric Cohen argues, however, that the research community is well served by the current number of federally approved lines. After reading these two viewpoints, which argument do you think is stronger? Explain your reasoning.

3. The Civil Society Institute/Results for America claims that the American public supports embryonic stem cell research; however, the United States Conference of Catholic Bishops claims they do not. Examine the questions each

organization asked its poll participants and identify added information or explanations in at least one question from each poll that might have influenced the way people answered the question. Do you think poll questions can be crafted to make certain answers more likely? How so?

4. What evidence does Gareth Cook use to support his assertion that stem cell research is lagging in the United States? What evidence does Do No Harm use to support its assertion that U.S. stem cell research is not lagging? Which evidence do you think is stronger and why?

Chapter 4

1. William B. Neaves argues that those who "pit" adult stem cells against embryonic stem cells are trying to mislead the general public. On the other hand, Jean Peduzzi-Nelson maintains that the general public isn't being told about the advantages of adult stem cells over embryonic stem cells. Whose argument do you find most convincing and why?

2. Based on your reading of the viewpoints in Chapter 4, do you think there are alternatives to embryonic stem cells? Support your answer with examples from the text.

Organizations to Contact

The editors have compiled the following list of organizations concerned with the issues debated in this book. The descriptions are derived from materials provided by the organizations. All have publications or information available for interested readers. The list was compiled on the date of publication of the present volume; the information provided here may change. Be aware that many organizations take several weeks or longer to respond to inquiries, so allow as much time as possible.

Center for Bioethics and Human Dignity
2065 Half Day Rd., Bannockburn, IL 60015
(847) 317-8180 • Fax: (847) 317-8101
e-mail: info@cbhd.org
Web site: www.cbhd.org

The Center for Bioethics and Human Dignity is a nonprofit organization established in 1994 in response to a lack of Christian input in the area of bioethics. The center promotes the potential contribution of biblical values in bioethical issues, such as stem cell research. The organization produces a wide range of live, recorded, and written resources examining bioethical issues, such as "A Review of *Stem Cell Now: A Brief Introduction to the Coming Medical Revolution.*"

Coalition for the Advancement of Medical Research (CAMR)
2021 K St. NW, Suite 305, Washington, DC 20006
(202) 293-2856
e-mail: camresearch@yahoo.com
Web site: www.camradvocacy.org

The Coalition for the Advancement of Medical Research was formed in 2001 to speak for patients, scientists, and physicians in the debate over stem cell research and the future of regenerative medicine. The group works to advance cutting edge research and technologies in regenerative medicine, including embryonic stem cell research and somatic cell nuclear transfer (SCNT) in order to cure disease and alleviate suffering. The organization publishes various policy statements and FAQs about stem cell research and SCNT, including *Myth vs. Fact. . . . SCNT (Therapeutic Cloning)* and *Alternative Methods of Producing Stem Cells: No Substitute for Embryonic Stem Cell Research.*

Do No Harm: The Coalition of Americans for Research Ethics
1100 H St. NW, Suite 700, Washington, DC   20005
(202) 347-6840 • Fax (202)347-6849
Web site: www.stemcellresearch.org

Do No Harm was founded by several scientists in July 1999 to oppose human embryonic stem cell research. The organization believes embryonic stem cell research is scientifically unnecessary, violates existing laws and policies, and is unethical. The organization acts as a clearinghouse for news and information on the dangers and failures of embryonic stem cells and the successes of alternative research. The organization publishes various fact sheets, background pieces, and reports related to stem cell research on its Web site, including *Diabetes Treatments: Adult Cells vs. Embryonic Stem Cells* and *Recent Advances in Adult Stem Cell Research and Other Alternatives to Embryonic Stem Cell Research/Cloning.*

Family Research Council (FRC)
801 G St. NW, Washington, DC   20001
(202) 393-2100 • Fax: (202) 393-2134
Web site: www.frc.org

The Family Research Council is a conservative Christian non-profit think tank and lobbying organization formed in 1981 by James Dobson. Its function is to promote what it considers to be traditional family values and socially conservative views on many issues, including divorce, homosexuality, abortion, and stem cell research. The FRC established the Center for Human Life and Bioethics in 1993 with the mission to inform and shape the public debate and to influence public policy to ensure the human person is respected in law, science, and society. The center publishes papers and other resources useful to the academic political communities as well as to the general public, including *Real-World Successes of Adult Stem Cell Research*.

Federation of American Societies of Experimental Biology (FASEB)

9650 Rockville Pike, Bethesda, MD 20814
(301) 634-7000 • Fax: (301) 634-7001
Web site: www.faseb.org

The Federation of American Societies for Experimental Biology was established in 1912 by three member societies. It currently consists of more than twenty societies, including American Society for Biochemistry and Molecular Biology and The American Society of Human Genetics. FASEB advances biological science through collaborative advocacy of research policies that promote scientific progress and education and lead to improvements in human health. The organization publishes a monthly peer reviewed scientific research journal, *FASEB Journal* and *Breakthroughs in Bioscience*, a series of illustrated essays that explain recent breakthroughs in biomedical research and how they are important to society.

International Society for Stem Cell Research (ISSCR)

60 Revere Dr., Suite 500, Northbrook, IL 60062
(847) 509-1944 • Fax: (847) 480-9282
e-mail: isscr@isscr.org
Web site: www.isscr.org

The International Society for Stem Cell Research is an independent, nonprofit organization formed in 2002 to foster the exchange and dissemination of information on stem cell research. The organization provides news and information relating to stem cells and promotes professional and public education in all areas of stem cell research. ISSCR publishes the

Pulse, a newsletter that provides information on the organization, stem cell research news, scientific and industrial meetings, and other items of interest to stem cell researchers.

Juvenile Diabetes Research Foundation International (JDRF)
120 Wall St., New York, NY   10005-4001
(800) 533-CURE (2873)
e-mail: info@jdrf.org
Web site: www.jdrf.org

The Juvenile Diabetes Research Foundation is the leading charitable funder and advocate of type 1 (aka juvenile) diabetes research worldwide. The mission of JDRF is to find a cure for diabetes and its complications through the support of research, including embryonic stem cell research and somatic cell nuclear transfer. The JDRF works to effect changes in laws and policies that are favorable for diabetes research and to provide support for the parents of children with diabetes. The organization also seeks to raise the awareness of diabetes worldwide. JDRF publishes *Research Frontline,* an e-mail newsletter that provides the latest information about research on type 1 diabetes and its complications, and the magazine *Countdown,* which offers in-depth analyses of cutting-edge research and new treatments, and also features the personal stories of diabetes sufferers.

National Institutes of Health (NIH)
9000 Rockville Pike, Bethesda, MD   20892
(301) 496-4000
e-mail: NIHinfo@od.nih.gov
Web site: http://stemcells.nih.gov

The National Institutes of Health, a part of the U.S. Department of Health and Human Services, is the primary federal agency for conducting and supporting medical research in the United States. The NIH is responsible for maintaining the Human Embryonic Stem Cell Registry, which lists the derivations of stem cell lines eligible for federal funding. The NIH's Stem Cell information Web site provides various educational materials, FAQs, and scientific resources. The agency publishes comprehensive reports on stem cell research–related topics such as *Regenerative Medicine, 2006.*

National Marrow Donor Program (NMDP)
3001 Broadway St. NE, Suite 500
Minneapolis, MN   55413-1753
(800) 627-7692
e-mail: tmf@nmdp.org
Web site: www.marrow.org

The National Marrow Donor Program helps people who need bone marrow, blood, or umbilical cord blood transplants. The organization maintains the largest listing of volunteer donors and cord blood units in the world, supports patients and doctors, and matches patients with donors. NMDP publishes the newsletter, *Living Now,* which contains a collection of observations, tips, and resources to help patients make the most of their lives while waiting for a matching donor.

National Right to Life Committee (NRLC)
512 Tenth St. NW, Washington, DC   20004
(202) 626-8800
e-mail: NRLC@nrlc.org
Web site: www.nrlc.org

The National Right to Life Committee was founded in Detroit in 1973 in response to the U.S. Supreme Court decision legalizing abortion. The NRLC is the largest pro-life organization in the United States. The group has local chapters in all fifty states and works to effect pro-life policies by lobbying the government at all levels. The group also serves as a clearinghouse of information and publishes the *National Right to Life News* on a periodic basis.

Stem Cell Research Foundation (SCRF)
22512 Gateway Center Dr., Clarksburg, MD   20871
(877) 842-3442

e-mail: info@stemcellresearchfoundation.org
Web site: www.stemcellresearchfoundation.org

The Stem Cell Research Foundation is a nonprofit organization dedicated to finding cures for a wide range of diseases using stem cells. Toward this goal the SCRF provides public education and funds basic and clinical stem cell research. The SCRF Web site provides information about stem cells, such as FAQs and newly reported research. The SCRF newsletter, the *Source*, provides updates, written in nontechnical terminology, about the research currently being funded by the SCRF program. It also offers other timely information about stem cell research.

WiCell Research Institute
PO Box 7365, Madison, WI   53707-7365
(608) 263-6297 • Fax: (608) 263-1064
e-mail: info@wicell.org
Web site: www.wicell.org

WiCell is a nonprofit research institute established in 1999 by the Wisconsin Alumni Research Foundation (WARF) to advance the science of stem cells. The organization focuses on enhancing and expanding the study of human embryonic stem cells by generating fundamental knowledge; establishing research protocols; providing cell lines, research tools, and training to scientists worldwide; and supporting other stem cell research efforts. WiCell is tasked by WARF, the holder of human embryonic stem cell patents, to maintain the National Stem Cell Bank, which provides human embryonic stem cells to researchers throughout the world. The organization also provides training for scientists and offers educational outreach programs for K-12 students and the community. The Wicell Web site includes a Stem Cell FAQ.

Bibliography of Books

Brian Alexander *Rapture: How Biotech Became the New Religion.* New York: Basic Books, 2003.

Michael Bellomo *The Stem Cell Divide: The Facts, the Fiction, and the Fear Driving the Greatest Scientific, Political, and Religious Debate of Our Time.* New York: American Management Association, 2006.

Laura Black *The Stem Cell Debate: The Ethics and Science Behind the Research.* Berkeley Heights, NJ: Enslow, 2006.

Andrea L. Bonnicksen *Crafting a Cloning Policy: From Dolly to Stem Cells.* Washington, DC: Georgetown University Press, 2002.

John Bryant, Linda Baggott la Velle, and John Searle *Introduction to Bioethics.* Hoboken, NJ: Wiley, 2005.

Eileen L. Daniel, ed. *Taking Sides: Clashing Views in Health and Society.* Dubuque, IA: McGraw-Hill, 2006.

Andrew Goliszek *In the Name of Science: A History of Secret Programs, Medical Research, and Human Experimentation.* New York: St. Martin's, 2003.

Suzanne Holland, Karen Lebacqz, and Laurie Zoloth *The Human Embryonic Stem Cell Debate: Science, Ethics, and Public Policy.* Cambridge, MA: MIT Press, 2001.

Judith A. Johnson and Erin D. Williams — *CRS Report for Congress: Stem Cell Research*. Washington, DC: U.S. Government Printing Office, 2005.

Ann Kiessling — *Human Embryonic Stem Cells: An Introduction to the Science and Therapeutic Potential*. Sudbury, MA: Jones and Bartlett, 2003.

Helga Kuhse and Peter Singer, eds. — *Bioethics: An Anthology*. Malden, MA: Blackwell, 2006.

Robert Lanza et al., eds. — *Essentials of Stem Cell Biology*. Boston: Academic, 2005.

Jane Maienschein — *Whose View of Life? Embryos, Cloning, and Stem Cells*. Cambridge, MA: Harvard University Press, 2004.

Steven Paul McGiffen — *Biotechnology: Corporate Power Versus the Public Interest*. Ann Arbor, MI: Pluto, 2005.

Jeff McMahan — *The Ethics of Killing: Problems at the Margins of Life*. New York: Oxford University Press, 2002.

Chris Mooney — *The Republican War on Science*. New York: Basic Books, 2005.

Jonathan Morris — *The Ethics of Biotechnology*. Philadelphia: Chelsea House, 2006.

National Research Council and Institute of Medicine — *Guidelines for Human Embryonic Stem Cell Research*. Washington, DC: National Academies Press, 2005.

Joseph Panno — *Stem Cell Research: Medical Applications and Ethical Controversy.* New York: Facts On File, 2005.

Ann B. Parson — *The Proteus Effect: Stem Cells and Their Promise for Medicine.* Washington, DC: Joseph Henry, 2004.

President's Council on Bioethics — *The Administration's Human Embryonic Stem Cell Research Funding Policy: Moral and Political Foundations.* Washington, DC: U.S. Government Printing Office, 2003.

President's Council on Bioethics — *Beyond Therapy: Biotechnology and the Pursuit of Happiness.* Washington, DC: U.S. Government Printing Office, 2003.

Bernard E. Rollin — *Science and Ethics.* New York: Cambridge University Press, 2006.

Michael Ruse and Christopher A. Pynes — *The Stem Cell Controversy: Debating the Issues.* Amherst, NY: Prometheus, 2003.

Albert Sasson — *Medical Biotechnology; Achievements, Prospects and Perceptions.* New York: United Nations University Press, 2005.

Christopher Thomas Scott — *Stem Cells Now: From the Experiment That Shook the World to the New Politics of Life.* New York: Pi, 2006.

George Patrick Smith — *The Christian Religion and Biotechnology: A Search for Principled Decision-Making.* Norwell, MA: Springer, 2005.

Wesley Smith — *Consumer's Guide to a Brave New World.* San Francisco: Encounter, 2004.

Nancy E. Snow, ed. — *Stem Cell Research: New Frontiers in Science and Ethics.* Notre Dame, IN: University of Notre Dame Press, 2004.

Jennifer Viegas — *Stem Cell Research.* New York: Rosen, 2003.

Brent Waters and Ronald Cole-Turner — *God and the Embryo: Religious Voices on Stem Cells and Cloning.* Washington, DC: Georgetown University Press, 2003.

Wendy Wagner and Rena Steinzor — *Rescuing Science from Politics: Regulation and the Distortion of Scientific Research.* New York: Cambridge University Press, 2006.

Ian Wilmut and Roger Highfield — *After Dolly: The Uses and Misuses of Human Cloning.* New York: Norton, 2006.

Glossary

Adult Stem Cells

Multipotent stem cells derived from adult tissues that generally give rise only to the different specialized cell types of the tissue from which they originated.

Blastocyst

A very early embryonic stage of development (about three to six days old) consisting of approximately 150–300 cells and composed of an outer layer and an inner cell mass.

Clone

A genetically identical cell, tissue, individual, etc.

Differentiation

The process whereby a stem cell becomes specialized into a specific cell type.

DNA

Deoxyribonucleic acid, the genetic material found primarily in the nucleus of cells that contains the instructions for making an individual organism.

Embryo

In humans, the developing organism from the moment of conception or fertilization through the eighth week of development.

Embryonic Stem Cells

Pluripotent stem cells derived from the inner cell mass of an embryo at the blastocyst stage that can generally give rise to any type of cell in the body except germ cells.

Fertilized Egg Cell

An egg cell (oocyte) that has a full complement of genetic material and is capable of developing into a human being.

Fetus

In humans, the developing organism from the eighth week of development until birth.

Germ Cells

Sperm or egg cells.

Hematopoietic Stem Cells

A type of adult stem cell that gives rise to all the blood cells, such as red and white blood cells and platelets. Also called blood stem cells.

In vitro

Experiments or procedures that are performed outside an organism's body, in a test tube or a petri dish.

In vitro Fertilization (IVF)

A procedure, commonly performed to help couples conceive, where an egg cell (oocyte) and a sperm cell are brought together in a petri dish in the laboratory to produce a fertilized egg that can be implanted in a woman's uterus to develop naturally thereafter.

In vivo

Experiments or procedures that are performed within an organism's body.

Multipotent Stem Cells

Stem cells that can give rise to a number of different specialized cell types, but all within a particular tissue. For example, blood-forming (hematopoietic) stem cells are multipotent cells that can produce all cell types that are normal components of the blood.

Nucleus

A part of the cell that is surrounded by a membrane and contains the DNA, or genetic instructions of the cell.

Oocyte

Female's egg cell, which normally provides half of the DNA to produce a human being or other organism.

Pluripotent Stem Cells

Stem cells that can generally specialize into any one of the over two hundred different types of cells found in the human body, except germ cells.

Reproductive Cloning

Using the somatic cell nuclear transfer (SCNT) procedure for the purpose of creating a living being that is a clone of the donor of the somatic cell used in the SCNT procedure.

Somatic Cell

An adult cell. A cell from a fully developed organism. Any adult body cell, such as a heart, skin, or muscle cell, that typically has a full complement of DNA.

Somatic Cell Nuclear Transfer (SCNT)

A process by which a nucleus from a somatic cell is transferred into an unfertilized egg (oocyte) from which the nucleus has been removed, and the egg (which now has a full complement of DNA) is stimulated to begin development.

Sperm Cell

Male germ cell, which generally provides half of the genetic material to produce a human being or other organism.

Stem Cell Line

Embryonic stem cells that are derived from a single embryo and are therefore genetically identical and can be maintained and grown in petri dishes for an infinite length of time.

Therapeutic Cloning

Using the somatic cell nuclear transfer (SCNT) procedure to produce an embryo for the purpose of extracting its stem cells and using them to replace damaged tissues in a patient. The SCNT-created embryonic stem cells will be genetically identical to the donor of the somatic cell used in the SCNT procedure, and thus they will not be rejected by the patient's immune system.

Totipotent

The ability of a cell to give rise to all the specialized cell types of an organism. Plant cells are generally totipotent.

Umbilical Cord Stem Cells

Hematopoietic stem cells present in the blood of the umbilical cord and which are collected shortly after birth. Umbilical cord stem cells are similar to stem cells that reside in bone marrow and can be used for the treatment of leukemia and other diseases of the blood.

Zygote

The earliest moment of human development, when the embryo consists of a single fertilized egg cell.

Index

A

The Abolition of Man (Lewis), 99–100

adenovirus, 20

adoption (of embryo), 135

adult stem cell research

advantages of, 192

as alteration of human life cycle, 104–105

as alternative to embryonic stem cell research, 189–194

avoidance of potential embryonic stem cell research problems by using, 192

blood diseases and, 197

Bush on, 134

fetal stem cells v., 204

as having limited research success rates, 199

human identity and, 105–107

human life pattern considerations and, 102–104

identification and explanation of, 192

juvenile diabetes research using, 45–46

limitations of, 197

as morally questionable, 101–102

as not an alternative to embryonic stem cell research, 195–200

psychological effects of, 107–108

questionable claims regarding, 32

successes of, 193–194

Advanced Cell Technology, 209

AFS. *See* amniotic fluid stem cells

Ahn, Curie, 208

Alliance for Stem Cell Research, 197

Altered Nuclear Transfer-Oocyte Assisted Reprogramming (ANT-OAR), 117–125

as mimicry of human conception, 121–122

as moral solution for embryonic stem cell research, 120–125

opposition to, 121–122

overview of, 117

purpose of, 118–119

Alzheimer's Association, 61

Alzheimer's disease, 54–57, 58–63, 173

American Association for the Advancement of Science, 79

American Diabetes Association, 42

American Medical Association, 198

American Society for Cell Biology, 203

American Society for Reproductive Medicine, 66

amniocentesis, 228–229

amniotic fluid stem cells, 227–232

Annas, George, 87

ANT-OAR. *See* Altered Nuclear Transfer-Oocyte Assisted Reprogramming (ANT-OAR)

Anversa, Piero, 34

Aristotle, 121–122

Armstrong, Lance, 115

Associated Press, 224

Association of American Medical Schools, 198

Atala, Anthony, 228, 231

McGowen Institute for Regenerative Medicine, 205

medically indicated directed family cord blood storage, 221–222

See also umbilical cord blood stem cells

Mehler, Mark, 57

Mendel University of Agriculture and Forestry, 176

mesenchymal stem cells, 215–216

Mill, John Stuart, 11

Minger, Stephen, 174

Moore, Mary Tyler, 47, 142

moratorium (on federal funding), 128–129

Morrison, Sean, 36

mouse feeder cells, 150–151, 176

multipotency, 25–26

Murry, Chuck, 34

muscular dystrophy, 149

N

Nathan, David, 52–53

National Academy of Sciences, 79, 84–85, 198

National Bioethics Advisory Commission (NBAC), 78–79

National Human Genome Research Institute, 100

National Institutes of Health (NIH)

on adult stem cells, 192

clinical trial rules of, 21

federally approved stem cell lines and, 146, 156, 171–172

human test subjects and, 21

as monitor and regulator of medical research, 128

moral acceptability of embryonic stem cell research and, 78, 134

on time requirements for basic embryonic stem cell research, 63

umbilical cord blood stem cells and, 215

National Institutes of Health (NIH) Revitalization Act, 129

National Medical Association, 198

National Research Act of 1974, 128

National Review Online, 135

National Right to Life News, 48

Nature, 33, 34, 198

Nature Biotechnology, 155, 157, 175, 181, 228–229

The Nazi Doctors (Lifton), 86

The Nazi Doctors and the Nuremberg Code (Annas and Grodin), 87

neurodegenerative diseases. *See* Alzheimer's disease; Huntington's disease; Parkinson's disease

neurological disorders. *See* Alzheimer's disease; spinal cord injuries

The New Atlantis, 77

New Scientist, 29

New York Times, 19, 49–50, 210

NIH (National Institutes of Health), 21

Nisbet, Matthew, 162, 167

Norsigian, Judy, 66–67

Nuremberg Code, 71

O

O'Farrell, Vince, 231

OHSS (Ovarian Hyperstimulation Syndrome), 67

oligodendrytes, 36–37

oocytes, 66